ROWLAND
A Heart of Sunshine

BY
CAROLINE WHITEHEAD

PUBLISHING HOUSE

151 Howe Street, Victoria BC Canada V8V 4K5

© Copyright 2011, Caroline Elizabeth Whitehead.
All rights reserved.

Without limiting the rights under copyright reserved above, no part of this publication may be reproduced, stored in or introduced into a retrieval system, or transmitted, in any form or by any means (electronic, mechanical, photocopying, recording or otherwise), without the prior written permission of both the copyright owner and the publisher of this book.

For rights information and bulk orders, please contact: info@agiopublishing.com *or go to* www.agiopublishing.com

Rowland: A Heart of Sunshine
ISBN 978-1-897435-54-0 (trade paperback)
Cataloguing information available from
Library and Archives Canada

Printed on acid-free paper that includes no fibre from endangered forests. Agio Publishing House is a socially responsible company, measuring success on a triple-bottom-line basis.

10   9   8   7   6   5   4   3   2   1

DEDICATION

To Christine, Kali and Austin. Michael, Bob and Carrie.
Forever my love, Nana.

ACKNOWLEDGEMENTS

This story may never have been written but for the encouragement of my long-standing friend, John Flynn, London, England, who prompted me to write a follow-up to *Surviving the Shadows*. John is shown in the photos below.

Grateful thanks to my friend, Odette Meurer, who diligently proofread the manuscript, guiding me along the way to get it right.

To Bruce and Marsha Batchelor, Agio Publishing House, Victoria, for their support and expertise in making this publication possible.

ABOUT THE BOOK

Author Caroline Whitehead meets her long-lost elder brother, Rowland Marshall, for the first time in 1991 when he is 72 years old. Rowland had heard about Caroline's existence when he was thirteen, but had been denied any details. He'd searched for her in vain for almost sixty years.

Clearly they have a lot of personal and family history to catch up on – characters, events and settings that portray an era and culture that few today could imagine.

Caroline tells Rowland of being raised as an orphan by nuns, how she was forced into war work in 1942, and of her struggle to exist on low wages and wartime rations. Her thwarted political ambitions, emigration to Canada, raising a family, and always searching for her roots....

Caroline reveals to her brother the existence of three other siblings – William, Kathleen and Elizabeth – about whom he was totally unaware. She tells him of their early lives in orphanages and how they managed to survive without the support of parents.

Rowland wonders why Grandmother and Mother had not mentioned these siblings on the one occasion they'd mentioned Caroline. Were there mysterious circumstances surrounding the children and why were details of their whereabouts kept so secret?

Rowland's boyhood vision of living with his sister Caroline becomes a reality when the two of them decide to share a home together in Canada. This realized dream continued for the next sixteen years.

Quickly discovering a quirky, humorous side to her brother's character, Caroline also becomes aware of identical telepathic senses that allowed two siblings who had been complete strangers to understand each other in their later years, sharing laughter, fun and sorrow. The strong vibes between them from the day they met were remarkable; they begged not to differ.

CAROLINE ELIZABETH ASHBY – HER HUSBANDS AND CHILDREN

MARRIAGES/DIVORCES BIGAMOUS MARRIAGE	CHILDREN
Antonio Capolongo m. January 1910 no divorce located	Marie Capolongo b. September 1911
Edward Rutley Pocock Marshall m. October 1915 divorce - Decree Absolute January 1926	Rowland Charles Marshall b. January 1919 * William Henry "Marshall" b. February 1924 [Later discovered to be son of John Brandon.] Caroline Elizabeth Marshall b. September 1925 ** Betsy [known as Elizabeth] "Marshall" b. March 1927
John Brandon bigamous marriage December 1919 no divorce located	Kathleen Brandon b. July 1921 * William Henry listed above b. February 1924
Percy E. Martin m. February 1928	** Betsy [Elizabeth] listed above b. March 1927 [Note: birthdate of 1927 occurred 14 months following parent's divorce. We believe her real father was Percy Martin.] plus 3 sons living

TABLE OF CONTENTS

First Meeting	1
The Owl Barn	13
Marriage	23
A Charmer	25
A Political Dream	31
A Wish Granted	41
Mother's Grave	47
Elizabeth: A Gentle Soul 1927–1993	55
Southsea	75
The Gardener	83
Delirious Times	89
Trips Galore	99
Herbal Madness	107
Year Round Santa	111
Closer To Town	115
Trip To England	119
William: A Born Gambler 1924–2007	123
Kathleen: A Stylish Lady 1921–2008	151
A Man Of Words	173
On A Downward Slope	179
Journey's End	189
Epilogue	203
About The Author	205

FIRST MEETING

We first met at Victoria International Airport in July 1991. As the arrival doors slid open so passengers could enter the luggage area, I spotted him quickly. Despite never having seen him in person before, I recognized his face from photographs he'd sent.

He was a 72-year-old man of medium height, slimly built and well-dressed. As he approached where I was standing, we looked at one another, then hugged and hugged as though never wanting to let go. His smile lit up his face from ear to ear; I felt as though I were being offered the heavens.

After collecting his luggage, we found my car in the parking area and from the airport I drove along Lockside Drive, to show him the scenic beauty of the mountains and ocean. I pointed out to him that the snow-capped mountain in the distance was Mount Baker in Washington State. With the sun shining on its glaciered peak, it dazzled the eye.

Still in awe of my visitor, with whom I would spend the next three months, I was at a loss for words. Sensing my inability to converse, he commented kindly on the scenery and said it was breathtaking, to which I nodded in agreement.

Fifteen minutes later, we arrived at my rancher-style house and

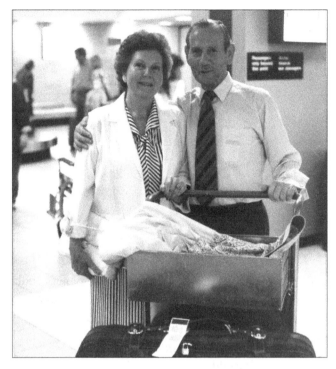

Above: Meeting Rowland for the very first time, at the Victoria airport.

Below: Showing Rowland the town of Sidney, near my house. Much later we would live together in an apartment in this seaside town.

parked the car in the garage. After showing him into the guest bedroom, I went into the kitchen to make tea. I knew he would be tired after his long journey from Manchester, England, so suggested that before he unpack perhaps a cup of tea might refresh him, and also a short rest would enable him to get his bearings. Ever smiling, he was more than happy to take this advice.

Meanwhile, I decided to prepare an early dinner and thought that after the meal my guest might like to enjoy a walk to Robert's Bay, a stone's throw away from the house. Robert's Bay is the oldest migratory bird sanctuary on the Pacific Coast. It is the wintering ground for bufflehead – a small hearty sea duck that dives underwater to eat from the mudflats of the bay. When the tide is out one can walk the length and breadth of the shoreline often seeing seals, eagles and other wildlife. It is a protected area and one to be treasured.

As we walked slowly toward the Bay I realized how fortunate I was in that this total stranger would be able to tell me something about a mother whose history was only partially revealed to me in 1989, after searching over fifty years.

Listening to a conversation between Grandmother and Mother when visiting Grandmother at Downham, Kent in 1932, my new companion had overheard Grandmother say, 'You've brought Rowland home, now why don't you bring Caroline?' When he questioned Grandmother about this person and asked, 'Who is she?' his question fell on deaf ears and all Grandmother was prepared to tell him was that she was his sister and being well looked after. And no more.

This, however, did not satisfy the boy's urge to know his sister. Yet Grandmother was not prepared to divulge her whereabouts to him, for some secretive reason. There was little the young boy could do. Upon returning home from visiting Grandmother, he put the same question of his sister's whereabouts to his mother. Her first response was he had no business listening to grown-ups conversation and that, secondly, the matter was closed forever.

As we sat on a log facing out to sea, enjoying the mountain and ocean view, the reality was slowly sinking in – this 'stranger' really was my long-lost elder brother, Rowland. But for the insistence of a genealogy researcher living at Whitstable, Kent, whom I hired to look into my family's history, we might never have met. While searching the indexes at St. Catherine's House in London, the researcher came across the birth record of a brother I never knew existed.

Once we made contact with each other in 1990, our letters traveled back and forth across many miles of ocean. I conveyed to him how desperate I was for every scrap of information he had on our mother, good or bad. In reply, my brother spoke with deep emotion of the short life he had with her.

At three years of age this vulnerable boy was put away in a convent in Sussex, England, and educated thanks to an unknown benefactor. He was told he was an orphan. When he reached the age of thirteen, his mother summoned him to her current home; her fourth husband wanted Rowland to work as an errand boy for the local grocery store and contribute to the family income. The relationship with the husband was always strained, and Rowland had greater ambitions so at the first opportunity, he enrolled in sea-training school where he would become a radio operator. Finishing his studies and passing exams with flying colours, he joined the Merchant Navy in 1936.

During World War II when his ship the *Waimarama* was blown to pieces in 1942 while trying to break the siege of Malta, he suffered third degree burns on his hands and face. Appearing before a panel of Naval doctors he was told that due to the seriousness of his injuries, he was no longer fit to serve his country. Receiving the news that his career in the Merchant Navy was abruptly ended at only twenty-three years of age, left him shocked in disbelief. He would now be expected to live on a disability pension of three pounds sterling a week from the British government, perhaps for the rest of his life.

At that time he was engaged to a young girl living in the Birkenhead area of northern England. How he would give her the news that he could

Taking a walk at beautiful Robert's Bay.

no longer work, gave him a feeling of foreboding. To be put on the scrap heap at twenty-three years of age was neither desirable nor something he wanted to face, but the reality was brutal and there appeared to be no turning back. When his fiancée became aware that his injuries were so severe he would no longer be able to work, and his service in the Merchant Navy was over, she retorted, 'I'm not marrying an invalid; the engagement is off.'

It was bad enough suffering with extensive war injuries, only to be slapped in the face by a fiancée who no longer wished to have anything more to do with him. She had neither sympathy or concern for him.

Undaunted, and with the help of his doctor who advised him to keep putting his hands in warm, saline water and exercise them with a soft ball, over months of persevering he was delighted to see his hands had healed remarkably well and regained much of their strength. Upon further medical examination by the Naval doctors, he was declared fit enough to resume his duties at sea. Needless to say, he wasted little time signing on another ship, eager to be back on the oceans, and seeing old friends, despite the wartime dangers.

Completing a stint of duty on the trans-Atlantic convoys, and due for shore leave, he and a couple of his companions went to a local dance and it was here he met the love of his life, Gladys. After a short period of courting, they decided to marry. The year was 1944.

After the war, my brother Rowland continued service in the Merchant Navy and finally left to join the Mersey Docks and Harbour Board in Liverpool, as a Marine Supervisor. He stayed with the company for many years before being forced to retire at fifty-four years of age, due to a war injury on his back.

Through his retirement years he and his wife travelled the globe, going from one country to the other, enjoying life to the full. It was always Rowland's philosophy to "live for the day" and he kept to that philosophy, knowing how close he came to death when his ship exploded, to the day he died.

Their idyllic life together, sadly, came to a halt when Gladys became ill while they were spending time together in their holiday trailer in North Wales. The diagnosis was cancer. It came as a dreadful blow to my brother when she passed away August 1990. He had spent forty-six happy years with her, When this occurred, he couldn't begin to think what life would be without his loved one, and felt his world dissipate slowly around him.

Still sitting on a log and enjoying the tranquility of each other's company at Robert's Bay, Rowland continued to chat, in a low tone, about our mother and his wife.

'Gladys knew I had a sister,' he said, 'but thought with the movement of people during World War II, that there wasn't the slightest chance we would ever meet.'

On board the MV Coho *ferry to Port Angeles across the Strait of Georgia from Victoria.*

Living in a fog of memories after the death of his wife, nothing could console Rowland's loss of a loved one. I was almost in tears when I heard him speak of Gladys's lingering death but said little, and continued to listen to his thoughts and watch his sorrowful expression. I wished I had been there to share his grieving.

In the following months, hardly knowing the time of day, or caring, he floundered in his daily life, wondering how it would all end, as his wish to live rapidly depleted. He could not see how life would go on without his Gladys.

Suffering with so much heartache he couldn't bear to live in the house they shared together, he put the property up for sale and went to live with his daughter and her family, a few miles away. Two or three

*Outside the famous Empress Hotel
in downtown Victoria, October 1991.*

times a week he made every effort to drag his feet back to the house to ensure the temperature inside was kept at a reasonable heat so it did not get damp, and to pick up his mail.

In December 1990, four months after the death of Gladys, he dropped by his house to collect the mail and picked up a brown envelope marked "The Salvation Army", London. Holding the envelope in his hand, he was curious why this organization would want to write to him. Upon opening the letter he was stunned to read, 'You will perhaps be aware of the work of The Salvation Army in the realm of family relationships, and especially in circumstances where for some reason there has been loss of contact. Your sister Caroline wishes to get in touch with you. Please 'phone our office on Monday, for more information.'

Hardly able to contain himself over the week-end, Rowland felt Monday morning could not come fast enough. When he rang The Salvation Army office and heard confirmation that I was looking for him he said, 'My emotions spilled over, I couldn't speak as the words stuck in my mouth and tears streamed down my face.'

Looking at him, I could imagine the scene as it played out over the telephone. One minute he was in the depth of despair and having to face daily realities, the next minute he was in a state of euphoria with news his long-lost sister was looking for him. The timing of this event could not have been more perfect. It was nothing short of a miracle.

I knew the feelings my brother experienced when he telephoned The Salvation Army office in London, because when David Wright, a family researcher, gave me the news he had found an elder brother I was overwhelmed to the point of disbelief, and couldn't wait for the day when I would meet him.

For months Rowland had been on heavy depressant medication to try to help him get over the loss of his wife but when he received news of my whereabouts, all the pills went down the toilet; he no longer needed them. Life for us would begin anew, and his boyhood dream, a reality. Desperately, I wanted to help him in any way possible to overcome his loss, but knew it was early days and the healing process would take time, if ever.

Throughout our three-month visit together we continued to enjoy the mountains and oceans on our evening walks on the beach where we would sit on a log, often in bare feet, talk and talk, like there was no ending.

I was forever saying to him, 'Have you noticed, we have toes and nails alike,' when our shoes were off. Then we would laugh and laugh, leaving me in uncontrollable fits!

One evening at the beach, chatting endlessly, I told him I emigrated to Canada in 1956 but the drastic change in winter and summer climate in Ontario where I lived, was so extreme I couldn't bear it, so we returned to England in 1959. My daughter, born in 1955, was ten months old when we arrived. When she reached the age of two, I left her in the care of a friend so I could take an office job at Gilbey's Distilleries near Mimico, Ontario. Throughout this period my husband was employed as an engineer at Coleman's in Etobicoke. I viewed Canada in the 1950s as a 'raw' country and backward in many ways compared to England. The laws were archaic, influenced by the early Presbyterians who frowned upon alcohol. If an adult desired to obtain liquor one was required to buy a two-dollar license before making any purchases in a liquor store, and be over the required age. Women were not allowed in the men's bars or saloons, and floors were covered in sawdust – a scene rather like one in a cowboy movie, including swing doors to go in and out of the saloon.

In Ontario, however, food was much cheaper and one could buy from Loblaws supermarket three chickens in a bag for ninety-nine cents. To grocery shop for a week, the shopper would expect to come out of the store with three large bags of food for the price of twenty dollars. Rents were cheaper, and jobs plentiful, albeit with low salaries.

Re-emigrating to Canada 1967, I discovered a whole new world before me, with strong development springing up everywhere. New plazas, housing, and a variety of supermarkets appeared. Sawdust in bars was a thing of the past, and so was the two-dollar license to obtain liquor. Canada was booming with a good economy. Life was great! My husband was employed at Hewlett-Packard as a facilitator until he retired in 1986. After studying accounting in 1969 I joined a Mississauga company as an office manager until retiring in 1987 – at which point we moved to Sidney, BC.

As we continued our walking and talking, we spoke feverishly about our mother, whom I decided there and then I did not like for the way she treated her children. Without question, I would have challenged her on the reason for abandoning us, if ever the opportunity arose to meet her. Rowland, always the understanding and compassionate man, with a heart of sunshine, would say to me, 'Don't judge her too harshly. We don't know what her circumstances were like in the 1920s.'

I wasn't altogether sure about this philosophy of his, as history proved over the years that many mothers throughout the Victorian era had many children but somehow managed to keep them at home, despite living under appalling poverty conditions. Grandmother Ashby had eight children whom she nurtured and cared for, until they were old enough to look after themselves. 'Why, then,' I thought, 'didn't my mother follow her own mother's exemplary behaviour, in the good Christian way she had been brought up?'

Our visits to Victoria, the Gulf Islands and many other scenic places were a delight for me to share with him. Every day was fun and laughter, which brought us closer together. Chatting for hours on endless subjects I never knew boredom or tiredness, as sometimes happens when you are forced to listen to a person who takes centre stage and goes on and on, without giving the listener a chance to respond.

While lazily relaxing on different beaches we explored each other's minds and thoughts of how life should be lived, and found a remarkable commonality in the simple things we liked and enjoyed. I discovered my brother had a talent for putting words into verse, and he never failed to surprise me with his intelligence on various matters, including his worldly travels. He could mimic different dialogues with such gusto, describing the people from whose tongue these words came, and have me rolling around in fits of laughter. I liked his African lingo best!

He spoke often of his life as a young man and related many stories of his experiences in the Merchant Navy during the war, which I found fascinating. The more I heard him speak of them, the more I coaxed him into writing a book, if only to put the record straight regarding historical events during the Second World War. He told me that some of the history written wasn't quite what happened to ships and men lost at sea, but to downplay the people's concerns, government press releases were written in a light manner.

All too soon my brother's visit was over and it was time for him to return to England. I drove him to the airport to catch his flight to Vancouver, then on to Manchester. Before leaving, we promised to stay in close touch and agreed to each write our own stories of how we had fared in life without parents.

I told him I'd jog my memory as far back to the age of seventeen and relate my experiences of events and ambitions in my early life. 'Good,' he responded, 'I'm sure it will make interesting reading.'

The hope that these writings would one day become a reality and make life more meaningful, made me conscious of the fact I could be overstepping the upper-class boundary mark; nevertheless, I pushed on, with one goal in mind.

Although I knew we would keep the promises made on both sides, my heart saddened at the thought that he was going back to his daughter and son and their families, and there could possibly be a glitch on the horizon that would stop him from returning. As I watched his plane take off from Victoria International airport, a trickle of a tear ran down my face. Three months of soul-searching and finding how close we had bonded, sharing the same interests, I knew I would miss him. I didn't want him to leave, and felt part of my life had gone with him.

Once Rowland's and my excitement had calmed down on both sides of the Atlantic, we became aware of our families' suspicions regarding our relationship. My family wanted proof and more proof of Rowland's bona fide identity before they would accept him. We did not anticipate this nightmare.

THE OWL BARN

I was seventeen years old and like many young people of my age, found myself working at Vickers-Armstrong aircraft factory in Weybridge, Surrey, doing my bit to help the war effort, which was mandatory under *The 1940 War Act*.

This *Act* also enforced conditions on every household in the country to make use of spare accommodation and take in lodgers. There was no choice whether an owner wished this or not; the *Act* prevailed, and if there was a hint of a house having spare rooms these were immediately seized upon by the authorities, who made the owner take in as many factory workers as possible.

Some of the girls were fortunate to live with parents, while most of us were forced to accept whatever digs were allocated, providing minimum food and heat. The camaraderie between the girls was tight-knit and whatever food they had, which was little enough due to rationing, they shared with their co-workers.

I not only shared a room with a girl named Lily who came from Ireland and worked at the aircraft factory, but we also had to share the same bed! One bathroom for five people in the house meant lining up, to get in. Emergencies of any kind did not qualify you, however, to jump the queue.

Days at the factory were long. You were out of bed by 5 a.m. and with a bit of luck managed to down toast, if bread was available, then charge out of the house to be on the bus by 7 a.m. where the bus put us down at the factory in Weybridge, in time for working the 8 a.m. shift. We would finish our afternoon shift at 5:30 p.m, arriving home an hour later, depending on traffic and weather conditions. Sometimes, when an urgent job needed to be done, we were asked to do overtime. This resulted in extreme fatigue by the end of the working day as we had been up in the early hours of the morning, with little to eat.

The winter months of the 1940s were particularly harsh and daytime temperatures barely rose above freezing point, so we were bitterly cold most of the day. With rationing enforced, to secure an extra bag of coal for keeping fires burning in the home was impossible. Each household received a quota of fuel, which did not last long. When overnight temperatures dropped to zero, we awakened in our bedroom to find moisture on the inside of our windows and outside frames glistened with hard frost or snow. To get out of a warm bed in the early hours, wash and dress for work, took a great deal of determination. When we left the house and had to walk on icy roads to the bus stop, extra care was necessary to avoid slipping and breaking one's bones.

I remember feeling terribly cold going to and from work and more so, on the buses, which ran with no heat. This coldness was probably attributed to the fact that we had little food in our stomachs, plus our lodgings were freezing, and we had to wash in cold water.

Our working week began on Monday and finished on Saturdays at twelve-thirty. There was no such thing then as a forty-hour work week. This was war, and every hour of production counted. Most of my wages, roughly thirty shillings a week, or if lucky enough to earn more by going out full on the production line, or doing overtime, were taken up with board and lodgings and bus fares.

Because of water rationing and soap being available in limited quantities, the lodgers were allowed one bath a week; lingerie and other clothing were washed also once a week, if a slither of soap was available.

In this situation, most householders waited until the following month before being able to purchase more soap, with allowable government coupons, while still being conscious that using more than the entitled water, was taboo.

The war held up hygienic rules, and many of us wondered when a sudsy bath would ever be made available, to indulge in the luxury of total cleanliness.

Despite working the long days and weeks, many of the girls would take the opportunity of watching the bulletin board in the factory for information on dances and other social events that were held for them at the Canadian Army camp located at St. George's Hill in Weybridge, Surrey, a short distance from the aircraft factory.

The history of Weybridge is interesting because of its connection to royalty as far back as the sixteenth century. Weybridge was once a small hamlet. Real growth started in the 1500s when Henry VIII built Oatlands Palace for his fourth wife, Anne of Cleves. Oatlands Palace was eventually demolished in 1649 at the end of the Civil War and all that remains of the palace today is a single gate in the form of a brick archway. Some of the palace bricks were used for lining some of the locks built when the Wey Navigation was being constructed in 1651.

On the St. George's Hill private estate in Weybridge, Beatles John Lennon and Ringo Starr are known to have lived there, also other famous names are Anthony Trollope, the satirist, Edward Lear, poet and writer, and other well-known artists. St. George's Hill was listed as the most expensive place to live in England and Wales. Houses cost an average of two to three million pounds sterling but obviously with today's market value, the price would be much higher.

The Canadian Army camp was housed on one of these large estates throughout the duration of the war. How the girls found the energy to attend these functions at the camp I'll never know, but we did, and with great gusto, thinking how sad it was for Canadian soldiers to be so far from home and no doubt lacking in female company – and nevertheless enjoying the time we spent with them.

Once the number of girls had listed their names on the factory's bulletin board, a jeep was organized to pick them up at a strategic spot in the town of Walton-on-Thames, not far from Weybridge. This orderly system of picking up young girls not only protected them from revealing where they lived, but also prevented the soldiers from being compromised.

Some of the girls were fortunate to be the owner of a pair of silk stockings, perhaps obtained due to a favour given to a Canadian soldier. I knew of one girl who wore gloves when she rolled her stockings carefully on and rolled them back down when she took them off. As the stockings were held at thigh level with a suspender belt on which hung metal clips, care was taken during the on-off procedure so that the clips did not snag the stockings. It was well-known among the workers that this girl's prized possession was kept in a jam jar with a tightly screwed top. For obvious reason, no one would dare pinch them.

The rest of us had to be content with using a liquid, brownish make-up, which was smoothed onto the legs, and smelled quite horribly. On the back of the legs a pencil line ran from the heel and high up to the thigh, giving the impression one was wearing stockings. If a girl was unable to get a straight pencil line on her legs, one of us would give her a helping hand. However when it rained, it was a blotched disaster, as the liquid joined forces with the raindrops that ran down the legs, taking the pencil line swiftly along with it.

Sometimes, when a girl found pieces of cardboard she asked the foreman of her department if she could be allowed to take it home. Going into and out of the aircraft factory the policeman on duty at the front gate checked all personnel, and if you carried anything it was thoroughly examined before he allowed you to enter or leave. Footwear was not the only shortage during the war and the very idea of being able to buy a pair of sandals was unheard of. To overcome this problem, with available cardboard in hand, I placed it on a flat surface upon which one foot, and then the other, was outlined on it, with a pencil. Using sharp scissors I cut the cardboard, showing a left or right foot, and with the aid of a borrowed tool, punched holes along each side. With rope or any other pieces of leftover fabric, I then criss-crossed the material into each hole, leaving enough length to tie a knot above the calf, below the knee. Once finished, the cardboard sandals looked like those worn by Romans soldiers, centuries ago.

Proudly showing the finished product to my sister Kathleen who was working temporarily at the factory at the time, rather than praising my effort, she remarked: 'Wearing cardboard sandals will give you flat feet.' To which I responded, 'Maybe.'

The cardboard sandals were serviceable during warm weather but when it rained, they became swishy and soggy. As I walked the appreciable distance to my lodgings the cardboard soles fell apart, bit by bit, causing the wet cardboard to fall away in pieces. By the time I reached my lodgings, toes and feet were bare, wet and cold, with rope or fabric hanging from my legs. I never attempted to make a second pair of cardboard sandals.

The camp caterers provided food for the dances and the amount placed on the tables had us continually gasping at the variety and portions being offered. I remember the dessert plates, the likes of which I had never seen and, believe me, would ever see again for a long, long time. Most of the girls tucked into the food as though it could disappear in a flash and ate to their heart's content. The generosity of the camp in not only entertaining us but provided a banquet at every function held, we were only too eager to accept.

There was, however, one incident at one of the camp dances when some wily character was intent on playing a trick on the girls. My feeling is that some of the soldiers knew what would happen and refrained from drinking the coffee, which was laced with Epsom salt. Unknown to some of the girls who were out to have a good time, they ate and filled their cups with coffee, only to find some minutes later there was a dreadful need to get to the toilet. By the end of the dance, stomachs were being held by the girls, who then threw caution to the wind, took off their bloomers, washed, and hung them out to dry on the branches of the trees outside the camp. It must have been a sight! This was one occasion I did not attend the camp's dance and after hearing what went on, was thankful I didn't go. When inquiries of the incident were made by the Camp Commander whose face was red with fury, silence prevailed, and no one had the faintest idea the identity of the culprit.

At this time in my life, along with several co-workers, I joined The Owl Barn, which was a youth club open in the evenings and week-ends. It was here we would gather mostly on the week-ends and play ping pong, also sit and chat while drinking tea round a large table in the main room. There was a small library, if one chose to sit quietly and read. Being a book-worm from my early days this is where I would head, before joining the crowd to catch up with the latest war news.

It was a great place to gather and be able to share one's concerns, knowing many of us were in the same boat, trying to make life more bearable throughout a disruptive war and make ends meet. Clothing and food rations were in limited supply and government coupons determined if and what you could buy, if you could afford the shillings. Many of us would barter for these items with coupons of any kind, thereby saving what little money we had. It worked well for most of us. Typical exchange might be, one shilling plus one coupon, for a second-hand dress or pair of shoes. If that was the extent of one's choice, that was it! We took what was available without making contentious issues and were glad of any addition to wardrobe, or stomach.

When a co-worker offered me a navy blue crepe dress for the price of two shillings and sixpence, plus one clothing coupon, I was delighted. The dress, of simple design, had long sleeves and a frilled-lace collar. The skirt hung just below the knee-line. I had one thought in mind – wearing it on occasions I went dancing at the Canadian Army camp or to the Playhouse in Walton-on-Thames, where dances took place Friday and Saturday nights. At each following event, however, the dress was beginning to look noticeably different from its original style. For example, the lace collar was removed and kept to make a much-needed purse in which to hold lipstick, of sorts, and a handkerchief.

Make-up being scarce throughout the war years, the girls would share what they had with co-workers. When lipsticks were reduced to a stub they were removed from the lipstick holder and each girl pooled her stubs which were put in a small pot to melt it down, with colours ranging from pink, red and orange. When this process was completed, the result showed the hot liquid with streaks of lightning colours. Before it solidified, one girl would meter out the warm liquid into each girl's lipstick holder. Surprisingly, once it set, the melted lipstick stayed on the lips as good as one bought in a cosmetic store. The colour, however, raised a few eyebrows, with a questioning look! Perhaps an unhygienic way of making lipstick, but it worked for those on war rations.

This method of replenishing unavailable supplies also applied to soap and in order to obtain something that remotely looked like a bar of soap, the girls would gather any slithers left over from either home or at the factory, if these were found discarded in the washrooms, and melted down in the same way as the lipsticks. When the bits of soap dissolved to a liquid it was then poured into a small narrow, one inch deep, four by two inches wide metal tin and once it set, one of the girls with a knife, would cut a square off for each girl. Armed with this luxury, we agreed to keep our secret and not divulge it to anyone. Had we known where to get wax to make candles, to help one read in semi-darkness, due to the blackouts, we would have gone full steam ahead, but apart from the churches using them, none were to be seen in the shops.

To give my only dress more style, with the lace collar removed, bit by bit the sleeves were taken off to the shoulders, and the hem shortened above the knees. The neckline, by this time, had plunged to a noticeable cleavage. The final assault on the dress was when I washed it in cold water only to discover to my horror, upon lifting it out of the sink, the fabric disintegrated in my hands and bits of it clung to my fingers. I should not have been surprised by this calamity which proved a point that nothing lasts for ever, but it left me speechless!

Our club house was a typical-looking barn but without lofts, where barn owls usually nest, with large gardens surrounding it. We had no idea of the name of our benefactor, perhaps a wealthy landowner or millionaire, who donated the building for a youth club. In the warmer days, we would make tea in the kitchen and sit drinking it in the garden. Over the months, familiarizing themselves with other members, many youths, boys and girls, would finally "open up" and discuss their dreams and ambitions for when the war was over. We would sit round the large table exchanging ideas and while some were of a personal nature, none of the members were judgemental in any way, neither would they dream of influencing you with dogmatic views.

Some time later, I was asked to become a youth club leader and was delighted to be chosen. Perhaps this came about because of my caring disposition and forever trying to help those less fortunate than myself. Being a people's person I was eager to help another fellow worker in time of need, despite having little or no money to offer.

At week-ends, club funds permitting, we would hire a rowing boat and for the fun of it, try to make our way up toward the weir on the Wey River. The boat carrying three or four of us was difficult to keep on course because as we neared the weir, the boat would suddenly swirl round due to the rushing water. Although we tried getting as close to the weir as possible we realized the danger of capsizing the boat and risking the lives of occupants. Being young and foolish we did not want to be outdone by unsuccessful attempts; however, providence warned that rowing the boat closer to the weir could prove fatal. Eventually common sense prevailed and no one drowned.

Often a group of us girls would go swimming in the river to relax, and enjoy the freedom of wailing sirens. One day, as we stepped out of the river to put on dry clothes, we discovered to our horror they were not there. Standing freezing in the cold, we muttered a few choice words and suddenly heard laughter coming from the nearby bushes. As we approached the area we found not only spectators staring at four girls soaked to the skin, but our towels and clothes hanging adrift on tree branches. Needless to say, we didn't waste time drying off and getting into our clothes, with sharp remarks to the mischievous culprits.

My experience as a Barn Owl youth club leader probably prompted the urge in me to want to become a Welfare Officer. I knew, however, this dream could never be fulfilled due to the fact I was lacking in education and any remote chance of finally getting a university degree was out of the question. Despite this, I had visions of the path I would follow once the war was over, and life became a normality. I was determined, somehow, to learn, listen, and keep educating myself in the hope that one day I would achieve my dream of success in political leadership.

MARRIAGE

In 1944, at nineteen years of age, I weighed slightly over eighty pounds and was rather skinny.

It was during a Saturday night's dance held at Walton-on-Thames, Surrey, in the 'High Spot,' which was nicknamed the "half-a-crown-hop", as this is what it cost to gain admittance, that a friend introduced me to a handsome blond in his mid-twenties. Clarence 'Larry' Whitehead was nearly six feet tall, and had been born in Glamorganshire, South Wales. He was a mechanical engineer, and employed throughout the war on essential war work.

We started to court each other and, within three months, decided to become engaged. Feeling extremely excited with this turn of event in my life, Larry took me into Guildford, Surrey, by train, where we selected an engagement ring of opal and diamonds at one of the local jewellery shops. The pride of wearing it on my third finger left me enthralled.

Throughout this period, although we both worked long hours in war factories, whatever time we had off at week-ends, we made the best of: either rowing on the River Thames, dancing, going to see a film at our local cinema, or meeting friends for a drink in one of the pubs. We were two young happy people seemingly without a care in the world.

After six months of courting, we decided to get married. Being under the legal age and with no known parents from whom I could obtain permission to marry, I was required to appear before the local magistrate at Chertsey Assizes in Surrey. Standing before the magistrate I hardly dared to breathe, but much to my surprise the ordeal went smoother than I had anticipated. The magistrate asked me several questions and appeared satisfied with my answers, while nodding his head. Consent to marry was duly granted. I left the courtroom, feeling elated, and could hardly wait to give my fiancé the exciting news.

The wedding date was set for the afternoon of July 29. I was dressed in a long, white gown borrowed from a co-worker named Eileen, who was also one of my bridesmaids, together with my eldest sister Kathleen. The ceremony took place in the Catholic church at Walton-on-Thames. The service began at two o'clock and finished at exactly ten minutes past the hour. Lighted candles, mass or holy communion was forbidden due to the groom being non-Catholic.

We had not long married when the British Army decided they needed him more than me, for a two to three years stint of duty.

Life for me moved on, always with hopes of a political future.

A CHARMER

In 1945 the Second World War was now over and factory workers were gradually making future plans despite food, clothing and gas still rationed, with the proverbial government coupons necessary to make these purchases. Many of the girls quit their jobs or gave up their uniforms. But they had nothing to do in the postwar era save factory work which was given to them because of their experience and training. Many women in the late 1950s were still employed in industry as welders and sheet metal workers. The rest no doubt married ex-servicemen and lived with parents because of the housing shortages.

Although it was crucial to be employed in order to support myself, I left Vickers and enrolled in a commercial college to train as a secretary. I was determined to succeed in my studies and hopeful that my goal to be involved in politics would become a reality. My thoughts were, first things first, achieve the extra curriculum, and go from there. After passing my exams I applied for a position in the Personnel Department of a Dental Company, located at Walton-on-Thames. This was the only factory in the district, employing most of the local inhabitants and looked upon as a good place to work.

In order to get a position at the Dental Company, one was required to undergo a finger dexterity test. Seated before my interviewer, in a small room, he placed before me a chart on which showed numerous puzzles. I was required a certain time to get all pieces of the puzzle in place. Nervous of this test, yes, but with mind on matter, I diligently put all the pieces together. Having finished within the allotted time, I handed the chart back to the interviewer who watched me throughout the process, then congratulated me saying, 'You've pass the test, with the highest score since the test was implemented.' I was delighted to receive such praise.

I discovered that my husband Larry had, at one time, also been employed by the Dental Company. When the sirens warned of an enemy air attack he was required to do roof duty, which left one vulnerable when incendiary bombs were falling all over the area.

The work at the Dental Company was interesting as each girl, four of us in Personnel, were given the task of following-up union complaints, housing, wages and canteen problems. Weekly, each girl would take up a different section of Personnel and report back our findings to the person in charge of the department. The company was noted for having strong union connections, representing all workers, and if a complaint was made this was negotiated between Management and the Shop Steward.

It was during this period in 1946 when a young, ash blonde came to work in the Personnel department. In her early twenties, tall and slim, she mesmerized the rest of us with her expensive clothing, jewellery and make-up. Her eyelashes were thick and long and I never knew if they were real or false as I couldn't get close enough to her to study them. She came from a well-to-do family and her father, Robson-Brown, was a member of parliament for the district of Weybridge, Surrey. Knowing her background, it was our impression that Jean, as she was known, could never be short of money, being a politician's daughter. Dumbfounded to the point of disbelief, we thought she was the one person ever to be in need of anything, but Jean surprised us all, using her charismatic charm, to sell illicit food and clothing coupons for two shillings and sixpence each, to anyone wishing to buy. How she came into possession of this endless supply of coupons, we could only guess.

'Surely,' we thought, 'she can't be that short of money.'

But, with pure diplomacy, any questions put to Jean, she responded with a dazzling smile.

Jean didn't stay at the Dental Company more than three months and one particular Friday, after work, disappeared without a word to the girls. Rumour went around that she had recently become engaged to a wealthy young man, so we assumed either this was her reason for leaving or, perhaps, she'd become bored with office work.

The winter of 1947 was extremely harsh, and many shops and factories in the area closed due to lack of fuel, and severe road conditions. The Dental Company was not able to provide workers with their jobs for at least a week. A girl named Fitz (perhaps short for Fitzmorris) and myself were fortunate to be kept on in the office throughout this period, specifically to assist those workers coming into Personnel to fill out the necessary forms, to claim unemployment benefit. Throughout the week I walked to work, gingerly stepping over ice and snow, and although wearing old woollies, scarves and gloves, was freezing with cold, between home and office. The nicest part of braving the elements was that I still received my wages at the end of the week.

In March 1949, clothes rationing ended in Great Britain.

Arthur Kenneth Perkins, an Industrial Psychologist, to whom we reported, was in charge of Personnel. He was a highly intelligent man who, despite his disfigurement, oozed charm. When speaking about him we used his initials, AKP, but showed every respect by addressing him as Mr. Perkins, when in his presence. Apparently, when a young lad of thirteen, AKP was doing chemical tests in his father's laboratory where they lived at Hove, Sussex, and while he was experimenting with different chemicals an explosion occurred that almost took his life. His face, hands and body were badly scarred. Seeing the extent of the scars on his hands and face, one can only imagine the pain and time it took for his injuries to heal. The burns, no doubt, must have been horrific!

When dealing with complaints in the factory, located across the road from the administration offices, we would find Boller, the man in charge of the Burr Department, in a panic. Hundreds of girls working the machines to produce burrs for use in dental treatment, for one reason or the other, would decide to down tools at the slightest whim and stop production, thereby reducing the monthly projected quota.

By the time the shop steward, who was the Union Convenor, and a Personnel girl arrived on the scene, the threatened strike action had simmered down. On one occasion, the reason to down tools was because there wasn't sufficient cheese put in the bread rolls.

When I returned to the office, I thought some people are never satisfied with what they are given, despite government rationing, and expecting full cuisine service. Mr. Murray, our Canteen Manager, was a marvel at stretching the supplies of food and went to extra length to ensure the meals cooked for staff and workers were nutritious and at an affordable price, even to the point of baking the bread rolls himself, which were delicious.

When listening to AKP one did not notice his disfigurement, only for the man he was; intelligent, charming and a delight to catch every word uttered from his mouth. He would meet with his staff Monday evenings in his office, on the upper floor of the building, with advice and encouragement on how to deal with various complaints at the factory level. The girls and I certainly learned a great deal from him. This advice, in later life, would enable us to analyze problems and make positive decisions.

If he became aware of any staff's frustration, over some minor incident, he would take that person to one side and smooth away the anger by saying, 'Think, within a day or two you will wonder why you ever got so anxious.' Of course, he was always right, and we respected his decision and advice, which he gave generously.

At week-ends he often hired a mini-van and took the staff to London for a match of tennis. Often, when strawberries were in season, we would be invited to his home where he and his wife lived at Shepperton, Surrey, and grew not only strawberries but other fruits and vegetables in their garden. Many times the girls would be given large, ripe peaches, perched on the top of each desk. We had no idea where these came from and of course didn't ask, but once we devoured the fruit and juice ran all over our mouths, any thought of wartime measures went clean out of our heads. AKP was not only a compassionate, caring man, but a remarkable man in many ways. When his staff had personal problems he would listen to them and offer advice. When speaking with him, somehow, it made the problem seem so unimportant.

No doubt, due to pressure of work, we were told one day that AKP now had an assistant. This caused a complete transformation in the Personnel Department, with rigid procedures strictly applied to all staff member. Our new boss insisted we address him as Mr. Peers. No one liked Mr. Peers, who was an ex-Army Sergeant and wanted to do the same bullying with his staff as he probably did with the soldiers in his regiment. The girls were up in arms with his new rules and realized what we enjoyed in the past with "our charmer," would no longer be the case with our new boss.

Mr. Peers was a tall, scrawny, thin man with light brown hair and long pointed nose. He didn't seem to want to trust anyone, and demanded attention when spoken to. Keeping rigidly to rules, we were not allowed to divert from working hours and daily tasks. It was a rude awakening to the girls who had been allowed freedom of speech, enjoyed Monday evening meetings, and spent week-end time with "our charmer", to find we were now working under a severe man, who never cracked a smile.

On occasion, when personal hygiene was desperate, I would volunteer to help out a girl by going to the local chemist for sanitary pads. We had taken it for granted that when this need occurred we had only to mention it to another staff member, to let someone know we would be out of the office for a short time, and where we were going.

The day I "flew out and flew in," I was stopped by Mr. Peers who told me to go into his office, where he proceeded to give me a severe dressing down, and said this practice of doing business outside office hours was not permitted. Asking me the reason why I left, I put the package of sanitary pads on his desk. Glaring at them, disdainfully, for several seconds, he looked at me and in a gruff voice commanded, 'Go back to your desk, and take those with you.'

The girls were within ear-shot of his shouting and decided to appeal to AKP Mr. Peers's decision not to allow staff to leave the office without his permission, despite the urgency of a visit to the chemist shop.

When "our charmer" heard of the incident we were all told to see him, including Mr. Peers, in his office. In his usual quiet manner AKP explained the situation to our new boss and said the girls had the right to request permission to leave and that this request must be granted. After the meeting we felt some satisfaction had been achieved and despite our dislike of working under Peers, "our charmer" would always be there for us.

When I left the company several years later, I knew I would miss the girls and AKP. Somehow, the rapport we developed was unlike any other I had experienced. It made working-life pure joy.

A POLITICAL DREAM

From the day I became a Youth Club leader, I knew I wanted to be a politician. The only time I can ever remember being involved in British politics was when a young man knocked on my front door and asked if I would help him in his campaign to win a seat in the local by-election. I knew of him, but we had never met. His family name was well- known in the tiny Kent village where I lived, and also in the House of Lords in London.

An eloquent speaker, uninterested in his appearance, this young man looked as though he didn't have two pennies to rub together, but as a candidate for this riding was confident he would get a majority vote and win in the forthcoming by-election, securing his life in politics and eventually find his seat in the House of Lords.

The House of Lords is not only a legislative chamber, but also the nation's highest court of appeal, and the Lord Chancellor outranks all other judges. When the lords are in session the Lord Chancellor sits below the throne upon a puffy, four-sided, crimson-covered ottoman. It is known as the Woolsack because it is stuffed with wool, in tribute to the wool industry, one of Britain's important export.

It wasn't until I emigrated from England to Canada, for the second time in 1967, that I took an active role in politics. I found trying to get between the cracks of British politics was not easy when I lived there. You needed to be in the upper echelon of English society, with an old established name, and have a financially strong background. Without these, you could never succeed.

At the end of Canada's Centennial Year in 1967, Prime Minister Lester Pearson announced his intention to step down and Pierre Trudeau entered the race for Liberal leadership. At the April 1968 Liberal leadership convention, Trudeau was elected leader of the Party on the fourth ballot, defeating some promising, long-serving Liberals including Paul Martin Sr., Robert Winters and Paul Hellyer.

Trudeau was sworn in as Liberal Leader and Prime Minister two weeks later on April 20.

In 1970, Quebec nationalists and FLQ (Front de libération du Québec) members had underground cell groups and wanted to create an "insurrection" (open resistance to established authority). On October 5, they kidnapped James Cross, British trade commissioner in Montreal, and held him as hostage. Quebec provincial cabinet minister Pierre Laporte, also kidnapped by the FLQ, was later found murdered in the trunk of a car.

Trudeau did not waste time in assessing the seriousness of the FLQ cells and although he enforced the *War Measures Act* to deal with militant terrorist faction rising up against the government, he was criticized for having invoked the *Act*. Although Quebec was not at war, Trudeau took these steps at the request of the Mayor of Montreal, Jean Drapeau, and the government of Quebec, to stop the general threats and demands made by the FLQ. There were, however, many vocal critics of the Government's action, including NDP leader Tommy Douglas, who stated, 'The government is using a sledgehammer to crack a peanut.' While the *War Measures Act* was in force, 500 people were detained; 467 were freed before being accused. In the end, fewer than 20 people were convicted.

The federal minister of justice in 1970, John Turner, justified the use of *War Measures* as a means of reversing an "erosion of public will" in

Quebec. Premier Robert Bourassa similarly conceded that it was intended to rally support to the authorities rather than to confront an "apprehended insurrection."

Cross was freed on December 4, after his kidnappers had flown to Cuba. On December 28, with the help of author Jacques Ferron, Laporte's kidnappers gave themselves up to the armed forces. How ironical, years later, to learn the FLQ had sent a message to its cell group holding Pierre Laporte, that their target had been accomplished. This message, received all too late, gave instructions about ransom for a hostage who had been murdered already.

After settling down in a house in Mississauga, Ontario, I kept pace with government politics at the federal, provincial and municipal levels. Although I arrived in Canada but a few months and was keeping up with daily news on public concerns, there was one issue regarding health that prompted me to write to the Hon. William Davis, then Premier of Ontario.

In his reply the Premier stated he was surprised and pleased that a comparatively newcomer to Canada would take an interest in government policies so soon after arriving, and that the issue I raised in my letter would be taken into consideration.

After writing to the Premier I began receiving literature in the mail of upcoming federal and provincial elections and the names of those candidates running for office, mainly in my area, Mississauga East Riding. Firmly convinced I was on track to achieve my ambition of becoming a politician, I put my name forward to help in many election campaigns. I fervently hoped this would give me enough experience finally for being selected as a possible candidate in a future election.

When elections were held in the Mississauga East Riding, I was anxious to volunteer and do any work handed out to me, to help the candidate running. Often working well into the evening at the campaign office, I was typing and doing stencil work in readiness for distribution of literature to voters the next day. On these occasions I did not get home much before midnight as it was important to have the literature available in time for volunteers to put on door handles, for voters to see first thing in the morning before they left for work, with enticement to choose our candidate.

On week-ends, within miles of the campaign office, volunteers would either be dropped off at a certain point or walk to where we were to hand out or drop off leaflets in a selected area. Our zones were carefully mapped out by the campaign manager. Having picked up my instructions for the area in which I was to canvass, I stopped at a road where there were high-rise apartments. This was my territory and the purpose of being there was to ensure that every piece of political literature I carried was dropped off at every tenant's door by a certain given time, then report back to the campaign office for further instructions.

Caught one day by the manager of a large block, I was seen sharply off the premises with the threat, 'Get off, you bugger, don't come back!' I was a little shaken, but determined not to be afraid of giving out literature to tenants in other apartments within my zone. I was equally determined to get the job done, regardless.

This learning experience I later related to the candidate's campaign manager who chuckled aloud, from the way I was describing the abusive language used on his volunteers. 'I'll bring up the matter at the next campaign meeting,' he said, as though to console me, which was not necessary. From then on it was decided to send volunteers out in pairs, for safety reasons.

Being a scrutineer at various levels of elections is a learning experience. The rules are tight. When voters enter the polling station one becomes aware of a distinct atmosphere that any sign of eye level toward the elector is construed as trying to sway the vote in favour of your candidate. This is definitely not the case. Most scrutineers are fully aware of the election rules and comply with all regulations, some of which might appear archaic; however, the purpose of being there in the first place is to ensure every candidate receives his or her fair count of the votes.

Over the years when appearing at the polling station as a scrutineer, I often felt we were not quite in the same category as the polling clerks or returning officer, but to complete an election campaign without scrutineers would give rise, perhaps, to questions relating to the count not being properly conducted. There is always a certain amount of tenseness at the polling station when the voting boxes are emptied, everyone seemingly hopeful their candidate will win. Scrutineers play an important part in the electoral system and are there to ensure every count is heard and correctly recorded, included those considered "spoiled."

I continued working on campaigns, volunteering to be a polling clerk, canvasser and scrutineer, even to policing the door where voters entered the polling station. The public, in general, do not fully comprehend the importance of a scrutineer who works tirelessly on election day, prior to the polling stations being opened to them. Regardless of whom one scrutineers for, it is of the utmost importance that all ballots be counted accurately, which is the full responsibility of the returning officer. Those working the ballot booths are not permitted to wear badges of any candidate's party, for obvious reasons; this applies also to scrutineers.

Prior to the ballots being counted, I listed the names of all candidates running on a sheet of paper and when his or her name was called, recorded it on my list. Having finalized the last ballot count I would telephone the campaign manager with the numbers, who put them on the office notice board. With this fast system of counting, as the ballots were called, it wasn't difficult to determine the winner even before the final ballot count was known to either polling clerk or scrutineer.

There was always an air of excitement working in any campaign office, that caused the adrenaline to flow. I loved the activity of being involved with people who knew exactly where they were going; the meetings prior to an election being called, the political gatherings, candidates' meetings, which I never missed, and when all the excitement died down to be able to enjoy parties given by the successful winner, the bouquets of flowers, but most of all the "thank you" cards which every candidate, successful or not, would send to volunteers. The rapport at this time, in the 1960s and 1970s, was exhilarating, and between candidates and volunteers, the working relationship was second to none.

In 1976 I was asked by the Mississauga East Progressive Conservative Association if I would take the position as secretary, on a voluntary basis. However, before the Association could vote me in, I needed to become a Canadian Citizen. Eager to acquire this honour, I appeared before a Judge at the Brampton office in Ontario and swore allegiance to Queen and Country. The ceremony took less than fifteen minutes. After paying the required fee I was handed my Canadian Citizen certificate by the judge, who congratulated me.

At this time when applying for citizenship, it wasn't necessary to undertake a written test requiring knowledge of Canadian history, the name of the current Prime Minister and Premiers of the Provinces. Today the system is much more complex and the cost to process an application is higher than it was in the 1970s. Many new immigrants living in Canada find it difficult when speaking poor English, and perplexing to complete and write the test.

Returning home after receiving my Canadian Citizenship Certificate, it was not my intention to pop the champagne cork but to realize how far I had come in the short time I emigrated to Canada and that the precious document I now held would enable me to accept the position offered as secretary to the Mississauga East PC Association.

One year later, after the Annual General Meeting of the Mississauga North Federal Progressive Conservative Riding, I was asked by one of the board members if I would take on the treasurer's position, while doing my full-time job, which I gladly accepted. This voluntary work is done on a one-year basis, when new executives are then elected to the Board.

I was totally taken aback, one day, when the same board member telephoned me with the news there was a by-election being held in my municipal district, Ward 3, and the candidacy was "up for grabs." He said, 'What do you think, would you be interested in sitting on local Council?'

My fast response was – 'definitely!' I had no qualms in pushing toward this direction, knowing one foot in the door enabled me to seek other seats later either at the Provincial or Federal level.

I'd had many conversations about certain local issues with the woman councillor who represented Ward 3 and hoped to regain her seat, and found she'd always been negative to my response. She didn't appear interested in what local taxpayers had to say and shrugged off giving advice, or help of any kind, in what I thought was a blasé manner.

With the news that Ward 3 was "up for grabs" and being urged to "go for it," there wasn't any question in my mind I could win this seat. I had the money lined up for a campaign and had the support of many key politicians. However, when putting my plans in action to my husband, the one person whom I thought would give me his undivided support, I got essentially a smack in the mouth, a negative response!

Disappointment knew no bounds. I struggled inwardly for days as to the course of action I needed to take but came to the realization that, without the support of my husband, I would be banging my head against a brick wall. It was totally unacceptable to me that my youthful dream abruptly ended without being given a logical reason why.

I wanted to run away. "Hell hath no fury like a woman scorned." Many attribute the quote to William Shakespeare but it actually comes from a play called "The Mourning Bride" written in 1697 by William Congreve.

The incumbent in Ward 3 was well-connected in the district and wealthy, so on election day she must have been shocked to the core to learn she was ousted by the voters who yanked the seat from under her. This spoke volumes to me about how voters needed a voice at council level and that the person representing them must listen to their concerns. The swift action taken at this by-election left me with the thought how quickly governments can change, candidates being replaced at the whim of the voters.

Although the municipal seat in Ward 3 had been won by another candidate I continued with voluntary work at all levels of government, when elections were called.

Being defeated by my husband, without even a chance to face the voters, did not mean I would not keep the momentum going, of continuing in political campaigns. In fact, the urge to participate became stronger to work for those already holding seats at the Legislature in Queen's Park, Ontario, and who campaigned to be re-elected.

When I first met Bud Gregory in the early 1970s, he was M.P.P. (Member of the Provincial Parliament) for Mississauga East. One of the nicest, caring politicians you could wish to meet, he had a smile for everyone, and was dedicated to the task of helping his constituents.

In 1985 when he became Solicitor General, he wrote to me, 'May I take this opportunity to extend my personal gratitude for your many efforts during my recent election campaign. Campaigns depend so greatly on the support of many volunteers, like yourself, and in so many different capacities. Your dedication and hard work on my behalf is very much recognized and appreciated. My successful re-election truly reflects the strong and valued support I had in Mississauga East. I look forward once again to being your representative at Queen's Park and further welcome any opportunity to assist where possible.'

In a card thanking me, he said, 'It was such a delight working with you, I almost hated to see the campaign end.'

Prior to moving from Ontario to British Columbia in 1987 I acquainted myself with the knowledge that Victoria, the capital of B.C, would be reasonably close to Sidney where I planned to live. Because of a larger population and the size of Vancouver I thought the government buildings would be there rather than in Victoria, which surprised me.

In 1987, the Socred party was in power under the leadership of Premier Bill Vander Zalm. One day I walked into his secretary's office and while speaking with her, suddenly the door of the Premier's office opened and out he walked chatting to another person. I don't know which of us was more surprised when the two of us came face to face, knowing I had not made an appointment to see him. Today, to think it remotely possible one could get even close to the secretary's office without an appointment, is out of the question. No doubt due to terrorists' activities worldwide, the commissioners on duty at the entrance are extra vigilant and screen all visitors prior to entering the building, so one never gets past the front door without approval, let alone near the Premier's office.

At this opportune time I asked the Premier if he would look into a concern I had with a specific issue. Listening quietly to me, with a charismatic smile on his face, he assured me he would consider the matter and advise me accordingly. I thanked him for the opportunity of being able to speak with him, and left the office with a good feeling.

A few days later when receiving his letter, I felt that the little time spent with him had been worthwhile. It made me conscious of the fact that unless the general public speak out on issues of concern, governments will carry on blindly making decisions without taking into consideration public opinion.

After meeting the Premier I began to take an interest in the Question Period held at the Legislature during the afternoon on certain week days. These sessions were interesting up to a point but when the Socreds lost and the NDP took power, there wasn't a great deal of political clout with which to listen. When the Liberals took over 2001, and I left the legislature building after one session, I couldn't grasp why so much rhetoric and time was wasted on simple issues that could not be resolved there and then.

At one Question Period that Rowland and I attended, the new budget was being presented to the house by the Finance Minister. Eager to get the numbers right, so to speak, from the horse's mouth, I began hastily scribbling notes in shorthand, when I felt a surprised tap on my shoulders by one of the commissionaires. Looking up at him, he tut-tutted under his breath and wagging a finger at me indicated, this is a no, no! I was even more surprised that he did not ask for my note pad so tucked it into my purse, and pretended to look all innocent.

Whispering to Rowland, 'Why are the general public not allowed to take notes, but the media sitting in the gallery to the right of them, can?'

Was it assumed the public would get it all wrong and give newspapers false information?

During one session in February 2005 Rowland and I were listening to questions by Joy McPhail, then NDP Leader of the Opposition, who was rudely shouted down by opposition members, bent on stopping her from speaking. But, like a real trooper, she was determined to be heard and have her say. I was delighted to have the opportunity of hearing this slim, red-head politician who showed the strength of a Trojan to her fellow members by ignoring their shouting, amid much bench-slapping.

As I continued writing to governments at all levels on certain issues, I was conscious of the fact that to get anything done takes months, if not years. A constant merry-go-round inasmuch that once a policy is in place, governments seldom reverse that policy, despite public pressure to the contrary. The rhetoric response of most politicians who perhaps neither have the time or care to give you a direct answer to a direct question, leaves one wondering why you bothered writing to them in the first place, because what concerns you, is not necessarily of importance to them.

A well-known psychologist in England once said to me, "Lack of communication leaves one groping down dark tunnels." I was impressed with these meaningful words and wondered why our politicians do not communicate with the public, as they should, and stop passing the buck!

Sadly, since television and computers are now the voice of communication in our living rooms, we have not only lost the art of conversation but many families have become dysfunctional due to this, which has resulted in many unsolved social problems.

When relating my political dream to my late brother, Rowland, he looked at me thoughtfully and said, 'If I had been with you, you would have had my full support and, without a doubt, succeeded.' I firmly believed him.

A WISH GRANTED

Throughout Rowland's three months stay with me in 1991, he conveyed a wish to emigrate to Canada. Since losing his wife, Gladys, he believed he could not settle back in England.

His words to me were: 'There's nothing there for me.'

This truly saddened me to hear what he had just said, which came as a surprise, knowing he had family, but it gave me the impression he did not want children's noise, although I realized he loved them dearly. Clearly the message I received, was that he wanted a peaceful life.

To choose Canada as a place to emigrate, delighted me, knowing he had travelled the world when in the Merchant Navy and a friend in New Zealand had begged him to "jump ship" and stay there, when on one of his voyages. His refusal to do this, as he told his hostess at the time, was because he needed to find his sister.

It was at some point in 1991 that we were fortunate to meet Lynn Hunter, then MP for Saanich Gulf-Islands from 1988 to 1993, at Tulista Park. I had known her for some time and while we were on the opposite side of politics, I admired her for the way she had things done. To me, she was a people's person – and, as I was to learn when meeting her, a good listener. I introduced Rowland to her, and she asked him where he was from.

Rowland replied, 'Birkenhead, England.'

After discussing the events of the day, and sunny weather, I then broached the subject of how I would go about getting Rowland emigrated to Canada. I explained to Lynn how Rowland had recently lost his wife and that neither one of us, brother and sister, had ever contacted each other until 1990. From the expression on her face I knew we had touched a nerve, because her questions to us came at a fast pace.

We told her everything she wanted to hear, how we first made contact, and met. After listening, she handed me a business card and told us to take along every piece of publicity that was printed in the April 1991 issue of *The Best Magazine,* printed in England, about our story, with the heading, 'At last, after 50 years, we've found our brother'. The letter from the Salvation Army in London, and the article in the *Wirral Globe*, Birkenhead, newspaper with the heading 'Oh, brother!' 'What a surprise!'

The *Wirral Globe* printed an article with the opening: 'A wife's dying promise that the future would not be lonely has come miraculously true for Wirral widower Rowland Marshall and his family. Just two days before she died of cancer, his wife Gladys told him that "someone out there" would soon bring him great joy.'

'Depressed and anxious after her death, Mr. Marshall could not believe her message of hope – until a few days before Christmas, he received a letter from the Salvation Army telling him that his sister Caroline in Canada was trying to make contact.'

The name on the business card, given by Lynn Hunter, was Alan Froese, Immigration Counsellor, Victoria. After thanking her, we said we would let her know the results of our meeting with Immigration and what progress had been made toward Rowland emigrating to Canada.

We wasted little time in visiting the Immigration office in Victoria and handed the card, given to us by Lynn Hunter, to a girl at the front desk, who passed the card on to Mr. Alan Froese. After speaking with him a few minutes, he referred us to Mr. Ross A. Byers, a counsellor.

As we sat before him nervously stating our case why Rowland

wished to emigrate, the counsellor listened attentively to our story while studying the article in the English magazine, which printed a full page of how my brother and I first met.

While Rowland spoke softly about the recent loss of his wife, then finding a sister in the same year, I noticed a tear run down his face. I touched his hand to reassure him, saying, 'It's all right, really.'

Whispering about his dying wife and that she had now gone from him, finally finding his sister whom he had known about since the age of thirteen, caused him to choke back the tears. I was close to tears myself when hearing him speak of Gladys and knew he was floundering in all directions, wondering which way to go. For a moment, it appeared that every spark of life went out of him.

After checking both our birth certificates, the letter from the Salvation Army in London and newspaper clipping from the *Wirral Globe,* and again reading the article in *The Best Magazine*, the counsellor asked many questions; was I willing to accept full responsibility with a five-year undertaking that Rowland would not be a burden on our government? I was more than happy to consent to this agreement.

When the question of finance was brought up, we assured the counsellor this would not be a problem for either one of us.

While we waited in anticipation for further questions from him, he looked at us and said the story we unfolded was so incredible he would put our case forward to his superior. He also went on to say that Canada was compassionate in helping families stay together. I was happy to hear this and thought there was every possibility Rowland's wish to emigrate to Canada would be granted. Meanwhile, the counsellor handed me a "Sponsor's Family Tree" form and asked that I complete it as soon as possible, have it witnessed, and returned to his office.

On October 16, 1991 I completed the Undertaking of Assistance form which I enclosed with my letter to the Immigration office in Victoria, specifying my acceptance to be fully responsible for the welfare of my brother.

I also emphasized that due to our age factor, time is of the essence, and it is important that whatever years we have left to be able to spend them together, preferably in Canada, as I was already a Canadian citizen.

In my letter dated November 4, 1991 to Alan Froese, expressing my thanks for the courtesy extended to Rowland and myself when we visited his office on October 29, I also extended appreciation to Ross A. Byers for his patience, time and understanding concerning my brother's request to stay in Canada.

There is no doubt that our government unbends its rule for a good cause, as was the case of my brother wishing to remain in Canada. Although Rowland made a request to Canada House in London, to emigrate, his response, for some reason, was left unanswered. Because of our unusual family circumstances Immigration Canada in Victoria were not only compassionate, but willing to assist in every possible way in processing my brother's application for entry into Canada. To this day, I am extremely grateful to them.

By December 1991, Rowland had been granted a Visitor's Permit, which enabled him to remain in Canada. In January of the following year he was required to undergo a medical examination, prior to emigrating to Canada. The medical documents were to arrive in Ottawa by the due date, January 31, 1992. We wasted no time mailing them.

Having complied with Immigrations' instructions to complete the medical documents, Rowland returned to England to finalize some personal business. In July 1992, he officially landed at Victoria airport. I couldn't wait to pick him up. There was much we had to talk about and how he would fit in with my life in British Columbia.

We loved the Robert's Bay area, to watch the wildlife, and generally chat about all and sundry. I discovered he was very much a swallow and loved the sun and warmth.

I knew my brother wanted to become a Canadian citizen but there was a period of time that was required to elapse, before this would be allowed. In 2004 he completed the application and on June 21, 2005, received Notice to Appear – to take the Oath of Citizenship.

On July 1, 2005, Canada Day, Rowland became a Canadian citizen. The ceremony was held at the Mary Winspear centre in Sidney, where he received congratulations and was presented with a certificate. We had much to rejoice. There was no turning back. His wish to emigrate and gain citizenship had been granted. It would be a new life for us both.

MOTHER'S GRAVE

In March 1994, Rowland and I were back in England, specifically to dig up more details on the history of our mother's past, as well as visit her grave at Margate, Kent. We were also anxious to see how Elizabeth, our sister, was getting on since she returned to the U.K.

Arriving at Heathrow, after an overnight flight from Vancouver, we took a taxi from the airport to Kent, and arranged to stay with old friends for a few days. The area in which they lived was within miles of where I was brought up as a child but my friends were not to know that, as I had never discussed my upbringing with them. What is more, they never asked.

When Rowland made contact and visited me here in Canada for three months, I poured out my heart to him about my early childhood in an orphanage and gave him some details on how the children were treated. He was all agog to see the place but I explained that the building had been demolished in the late 1970s, as well as the adjacent Holy Innocents Church, where the children and local parishioners attended religious services.

On the day we scheduled a visit we caught the bus from the bottom of the road where our friends lived, and got off at a stop near the hospital, on Sevenoaks Road. Opposite the hospital, where the orphanage once stood, we found in its place the development of a large sprawled-out housing estate. Any notion that an orphanage built in 1894 and once ruling the lives of hundreds of children, was gone, with its past long vanished in the history books.

Showing Rowland where injured Canadian soldiers were treated during World War One at Orpington Hospital, I told him of one Canadian whom I knew well and frequently visited with his family in Scarborough, Ontario, whose leg was amputated at this hospital. "Pop" as he was known and I became good friends and we often chatted about the "men in blue." When they went into the village, local people recognized the soldiers by the colour of their uniform clothing.

Orpington during my childhood was a close-knit community where Sundays were kept strictly for morning services held at local churches, after which families united for Sunday dinners, perhaps later attending an evening service. The strict laws of the Sabbath were kept to preserve a religious day of rest, and to hear the sound of an outside lawn mower or to raise a sewing or knitting needle, was deemed sacrilegious.

We slowly crossed over Sevenoaks Road and walked gingerly up the long driveway looking this way and that to try and get our bearings, but whichever way we went I could not recognize the area I had known as a child. At the top of the driveway we took a right-hand turn and I spotted what was once the playground, and the old school house. Although the playground had been reduced to half its size since I played netball there as a young girl, it was still used by the local school children for exercise and sport.

The school house, now classified as a Primary Elementary school for the education of local Catholic children, looked the same as I remembered it, except that instead of nuns pupils are now taught by qualified teachers.

Walking through the newly-developed housing estate was like going into a maze of passageways, as they intertwined to such a degree that each house overshadowed the other, with minimum space in between, looking identical to one another. Each avenue appeared to go into another, causing confusion, as to where the entrance began and where it finished, with the result we were going round in circles.

Almost at a desperation state of being utterly lost we noticed a man passing by, who looked like a gardener. Explaining to him the predicament in which we found ourselves, he guided us out of the avenues. Laughing, he said, 'It's a bit of a mess trying to get in and out of the estate, but don't worry, you're not the only ones with the problem.' And he added, 'No doubt, they'll be many more to come.'

I asked him what happened to the little cemetery, near the playing fields, where I played field hockey and got walloped more than once on the ankles from the best team, determined to win. He told us the cemetery had been removed for the housing development and all the bodies were re-buried to a site in the garden in front of the new, ultra-modern church which opened in 1981. I thought this rather sad as I knew some of the children and adults who had been buried there years ago, including one six-year-old little girl named Monica who caught scarlet fever and died.

Happy to give us further information, the gardener told us that as part of the deal between the Southwark Diocese and the developers, an agreement was reached between the two parties to build a convent house for the five remaining elderly sisters, all of whom are Irish. The location of the convent is on Bishop Butt Close.

In 1877 Bishop John Butt founded The Southwark Diocesan Education Council and Rescue Society for the protection of poor and neglected children from South London, Kent, Surrey and Sussex. In 1891 a 60-acre site at Orpington was put up for public auction but did not reach its reserve figure. Bishop Butt was attracted by the opportunity, and the following day the Society purchased the land. This land was ultimately sold by the Society to developers in the 1980s, for the building of a large housing estate. No doubt, the Society received a handsome profit from the developers for the sale of this property, as well as acquiring a new house for the five sisters.

As Bishop of Southwark, John Butt was involved in the Catholic Canadian Emigration Society, founded in the early 1880s. This body funded and developed three homes in Canada, including one called St. Joseph's, at Hintonburg near Ottawa. Later the name changed to New Orpington Lodge. The second home was St. Anne's, for girls, based in Montreal; the third was a training centre for young men between 16 and 21 years of age, called New Southwark Farm, located at Makinak in Manitoba.

Thanking the gardener for his information we then walked back down the long driveway to catch the bus back to our friend's house. Before arriving Rowland suggested we stop and eat at one of the local pubs, so we could relax and talk. At this point we had not enlightened our friends of the reason why we wanted to see the housing development on Sevenoaks road, but that news would come later.

The following day our next stop was to see sister Elizabeth and our younger brother, William, who lived at Waterlooville, Hampshire, where we stayed with him for a few days. The last time I saw Elizabeth was to say goodbye to her at Victoria International airport when she returned to England, primarily to go to Rugby where she had, as she put it, a calling. Sadly for her, this expectation never became a reality, due to her poor health, so she was forced to live back in Hampshire, in a somewhat meaningless life.

When we arrived at her tiny flat that belonged to the local Council, we were shocked by the living conditions; bare, cold, and as far as we could see, lacked all home comforts. My sister, as usual, took life in her stride and never yearned for material possessions, and never complained with her lot.

After giving her big hugs, and having a cup of tea, Rowland and I sized up her financial position and forthwith decided to do some much-wanted shopping. We checked her food cupboard but like old Mother Hubbard, found it bare. Looking at Elizabeth we noticed she had lost weight and her countenance was anything but happy. I sensed her disappointment at not being able to fulfil her dream of doing God's work; however, the die was already cast, and I believe long before she left Canada.

Following a short visit with Elizabeth, William bade us goodbye as he wanted to get back home to his family. We linked arms with Elizabeth, Rowland on one side of her, me on the other, and walked into town. First to buy a small rug, then large coloured cushions, candles and anything else we could find to "dolly-up" her small living-room. Next, we concentrated on the larder, and bought endless amounts of food that we hoped would last her a considerable time.

Looking on while we touched up her place, Elizabeth gave a weak smile. I thought she was perhaps a little happier now that we were with her, and that she found the flat looked more home-like and colourful. Her words of appreciation fell on deaf ears as we felt what little we did, was not sufficient. We desperately wanted to make life easier for her. Before we headed back to our friends in Kent, we told Elizabeth we will be visiting Mother's grave in Margate in a couple of days. This seemed to please her but due to her health condition, we knew she would be unable to make the journey with us.

While I was reluctant to leave, and wanted to spend more time with Elizabeth, I realized that during the short time we were in England I was desperate to fulfill the journey of a lifetime I was about to make with Rowland, and that we would not dream of returning to Canada without seeing our mother's resting place. Also, at the back of my mind, I reasoned, if we don't do it now, there may never be another opportunity.

Our journey by train to Margate, Kent, was hardly a picnic. The railway station was freezing cold, the temperature, icy, and we seemed to have waited hours at Orpington for the train going to Tunbridge Wells. Arriving there, we then changed on to another train going southeast to Margate, only to find the train stopped, mid-track, to repair some default on the line. Finally arriving at Margate Station we stepped down onto the platform and looking around, discovered we were the only two passengers to get off the train.

As we left the station a slight mist was falling, and without umbrellas, it looked as though it wouldn't be long before we were both drenched. Hurrying along the Margate shoreline toward the town centre we hugged into our coats to keep off the rain and a strong wind that lashed at our faces, while watching high waves ferociously pound the shore; neither human or birds were to be seen. We were cold, hungry and frozen.

'Dear, God,' I muttered, 'what on Earth made us come here on such a horrible day?'

To which Rowland replied with his usual philosophy, 'Hobson's choice.'

Reaching the town centre, feeling somewhat deflated, I said to Rowland, 'Let's get a cup of tea or coffee.'

Luck, however, was not on our side. When we arrived in the town we discovered all the stores were closed for half a day. As we looked around, we saw what looked like a restaurant and opening the door, were surprised to see a crowd of business men, all suitably attired, listening to a politician named Edwina Curry, also known as the "egg lady."

Outspoken and controversial, she was first elected Conservative Party MP in 1983. A Junior Health Minister for two years she resigned in 1988 over the controversy over salmonella in eggs. She lost her seat in 1997. Her claim that "most of the egg production in this country, sadly, is now affected with salmonella" sparked outrage among farmers and egg producers and caused egg sales in the country to rapidly decline. Perhaps to get their own back on her one of the Egg Boards created a dish called curried eggs.

We apologized for the intrusion and told her we were looking for a place to eat, but nothing in the town appeared to be open. Welcoming us with outstretched arms, the speaker called out, 'Come in, and join us.' We thanked her for the invitation but told her we were on a journey from Canada and wished to visit a cemetery without too much delay.

'Try the restaurant on the upper floor of the British Home Stores, you might be able to get something to eat there,' said the lady speaker.

Thanking her, we left the building and walked toward the store, only to find the restaurant wasn't open. However Rowland, with his usual big smile, when he explained to a staff member we had travelled most of the morning to get to Margate and were hungry, she put us at a table in the closed restaurant and fed us fish and chips; the worst we had ever tasted.

To use a pun, Rowland chipped in, 'Beggars can't be choosers.'

And, typically, he over-tipped our server.

Unaware of the locality, and still freezing cold, we hailed a taxi to take us to St. John's cemetery and told the driver we had specially made a trip from Canada, to find our mother's grave. The young man was more than willing to help. On all fours, the three of us looked up and down the graveyard, when finally the driver stood up and said, 'I think this is the one you want.'

Rowland checked the number and said, 'Yes, it is, thank you.'

Looking down at a discreet number, it saddened us to think that mother's husband had not placed a headstone on her grave. Rowland and I wondered aloud if our lives might have been richer, had we been able to find our mother before she passed on. Knowing of Rowland's whereabouts, and the fact we both survived a rough childhood upbringing, she might just have extended love and affection to us. But as is known in our family history, this was not meant to be.

Rowland thanked our driver for his help and generously tipped him, then we headed back to Kent, and home to Canada.

ELIZABETH: A GENTLE SOUL 1927–1993

My darling sister Elizabeth was two years younger than me. A fragile person, she was never strong. Unlike me, with boundless energy, when a child, she was not allowed to do manual work of any kind. I believe her health condition was probably due to poor nutrition from the time of birth, as our mother's life lacked the everyday necessities when she lived in abject poverty in the 1920s.

As Elizabeth and I grew up in the same orphanage, there was a strong bond between us. I always wanted to be her protector not only because I loved her, but her lack of strength worried me. Her one aim in life was to nurse the young and elderly, with her on-going philosophy that people in their mid-age were capable of looking after themselves.

Elizabeth was demure, of average height, and had straight brown hair. Being brought up Catholic, she never questioned the Bible's theology or the hierarchy of the Church. Her religious beliefs were resolute and you could never argue doctrine with her even though I tried several times. A stubborn person who refused to budge on any issue once she formed an opinion, regardless of what valid view you had, she pooh-poohed your ideas. Her views were strong and because of this, I sometimes thought she had gone into the soul of an analyst. But we did amicably agree when political issues came to the fore and discussed at great length the virtues of those politicians who were in power, ostensibly to serve us.

Elizabeth was an avid reader and spent hours at her local library browsing through book after book, digesting anything that appealed to her. She was well-read, and her knowledge of world affairs surprised me. She knew many people in high places, also at her church where religious and social activities took place. I clearly remember that as a child she was never without a book. Often tucked away in the corner of a room, she would quietly read and not disturb a soul.

I had lived in Canada since 1967 in Ontario, then moved to British Columbia in 1987. I hadn't long been in my new home when my sister wrote saying she would like to emigrate to Canada. I was of course delighted with this decision, as I realized living on her own with a small pension was a struggle for her to make ends meet. What was more, I wanted to have her living close by so that I could look after her.

Elizabeth lived in London most of her life, working at different hospitals and nursing homes and because her earnings were so small, life wasn't exactly a bed of roses. She loved London with all its activities and meeting many interesting people from all walks of life. I didn't think she would ever want to leave it, or her friends. But I was wrong.

Accommodation in London, at best, is mainly comprised of flats, or Grace and Favour apartments if you were lucky enough to qualify for one, when retired from royal duties. On one visit to my sister's flat, I noticed with disgust the sight of chicken bones thrown down onto her patio from a high concrete wall, above road level. Elizabeth did not seem unnecessarily concerned when I commented on the chicken bones and rather off-handedly commented, 'It's from the tribe above,' but she didn't elaborate.

'What tribe,' I thought, 'and why were they in London?'

On one of my many visits to England I was met at Heathrow Airport by Elizabeth and we travelled the underground train to Kensington, where she lived in a flat on Stanford Road.

Not wishing her to go to the trouble of cooking I suggested that

Elizabeth as a young nurse, 22 years old, in London, England.

maybe we could find a pub, later on, for a light meal. She agreed this was a good idea.

Resting a while after my long journey from British Columbia, we chatted for a bit with latest family news. Later in the evening, we left her building and as we turned off into another street I noticed on the corner there was a house so heavily barricaded with security sensors, top to bottom, and loud barking from dogs, I asked my sister if she knew the occupants.

Her answer was, 'No, but I know the house is occupied by the family of the former monarchy of Iran, the Shah of Persia.'

As we walked farther along the road we saw a group of young people shouting and throwing bottles at barricaded windows of a tall building, tucked in a corner from the roadway. I could see they were an agitated crowd and I was not intent on being involved in their cause.

I took my sister by the arm and said, 'Let's get away from this place before the police arrive. It's not safe here.'

'Oh, I'm used to this, they won't attack me,' Elizabeth chuckled.

'How can you be so sure?' I asked. Was she that convinced her guardian angel would always be protecting and watching over her, to keep her safe? I hoped so.

The ruckus was outside the Iranian Embassy; the crowd, ugly. I didn't stop to find out what it was all about!

Hurrying away from the area I thought if this isn't living dangerously, I don't know what is. To cap it all, as we walked along the pavement I noticed several undesirables lurking in doorways, smoking what smelled like Turkish tobacco. I pulled my sister to the centre of the road and whispered, 'I'm not taking a chance of being grabbed by one of them.'

Laughing, and obviously finding my concern unnecessary, my sister responded, 'This is Kensington, not the East End of London.'

'I'd feel a lot safer in the East End,' I said.

I had met many caring people over the years in that part of London willing to help a total stranger, rather than those known to my sister whom she considered "the tribe."

Elizabeth knew many interesting people in London and introduced me to a friend who was a monk at Westminster Abbey. We chatted for a few minutes with him, then attended a service. Another was a baroness, beautiful and charming, whose appearance was immaculate. I don't know from which part of the world she came, but I was fascinated with her accent and elegant clothes.

At right, Elizabeth in her early thirties in London.

Below, Elizabeth loved walks in the London area gardens.

In May 1981 Elizabeth, who belonged to a Catholic church group in London, was invited to go with them on a pilgrimage tour to Lourdes and visit the grotto, where miraculous cures have worked since our Lady of Lourdes appeared to St. Bernadette in 1858. She was ecstatic to be given the opportunity of seeing in person this one place of which she had dreamed. In a polacolour photo, with mountainous views in the background, she is standing, smiling. After her trip we met in London and the first thing she gave me was not only the photograph but a tiny statue of the Virgin Mary, which I treasure to this day.

At one time when visiting her in England, she invited me to join her for mass at the little Spanish chapel in the West End of London. Before the service Elizabeth spoke to several nuns dressed in black, with the same colour headgear, which I found unusual, and introduced them to me. After the service she chatted to a number of people whom she knew, and appeared to be in her element among the crowd. She told me of a sixty-year-old count whom she met on several occasions at the chapel, and had given her two lovely Spanish fans. When she asked me if I would like to have them I was 'over the moon,' while in the same breath, was reluctant to accept a beautiful gift. 'But,' she persisted, 'please have them.' As she was to tell me at a later date, the demise of the Spanish count resulted when he died swimming in the ocean, somewhere in Spain. 'He was a good man,' said my sister, 'I'm sure he's now in heaven.'

Another friend named Dorothy was ninety years of age, living in a Grace and Favour apartment in Kensington. On the day we visited her, as we approached the elevator my sister pointed out to me a gentleman standing in the lobby and whispered, 'That's John Loder, the actor.' What was he doing living in a Grace and Favour building, I wondered. I was of the opinion these places were reserved only for those who served royalty.

Dorothy lived on the upper floor in a well-furnished apartment. She showed us some beautiful embroidery she was working on, for cushions and table centres, then served us tea on delicate china and silverware. She was as elegant as the baroness, and I was enthralled when she spoke about her life in the armed forces, serving as an officer. A delightful person, highly intelligent, I wished we had more time to extend our visit with her.

Elizabeth, despite living on a small income, was notorious for buying concert or theatre tickets for the same day I arrived, after travelling a sixteen-hour journey from Western Canada to England. I realized her heart was in the right place and appreciated her doing what she did, but being dog-tired all I wanted to do was sleep; however my sister was all agog to take me to a show. Surprisingly, once we arrived at the theatre to watch a ballet, or listen to a concert at the Albert Hall, I seemed to absorb new energy and forget my tiredness and enjoyed the show.

Like me, my sister was besotted with classical music at an early age. Often at a concert at the Albert Hall, or the Festival Hall, we would have to sit and listen to types of music I found heavy and boring. Chamber music, being one, did not appeal to me. If, however, Sir Malcolm Sargeant was conducting I would suffer souls gladly to watch him conducting the BBC Symphony Orchestra, while waiting to listen to a favourite piece of music by composers such as Sibelius, Ravel, Beethoven, Tchaikovsky or Strauss.

After spending a few days together in London, shopping around Kensington or going to Portobello Market, we would take the train to Hampshire and visit our brother William and his family. William was a happy-go-lucky sort who'd joined the Royal Navy at the age of seventeen. He wasn't the type to stand on ceremony, and expected people to take him for the person he was. His three children adored their Aunt Elizabeth, whose kindness knew no bounds whenever she visited them, despite having little money for herself.

It was fortunate for my sister that she didn't have to travel far from Kensington to get to Canada House in Trafalgar Square, where she applied for immigration to Canada. After completing the necessary forms and undergoing a medical examination as required for entry into the country, some weeks later she was advised her application had been granted. When she received this news my sister set about disposing of her worldly goods, albeit, few and far between, then booked a flight to British Columbia. When she telephoned with the news that her application at Canada House had gone without flaws, I was ecstatic!

In 1988, on the day of arrival, I virtually "flew" to Victoria International airport to pick her up. When we saw each other I wasn't surprised to see her looking totally worn out by the long journey; nevertheless, we exchanged huge hugs. She smiled at me, weakly.

Most of us who travel across the Atlantic ocean are aware what flying does to the system, but a good long rest inevitably cures the jet-lag.

Elizabeth stayed a month with me and, like Rowland, loved Robert's Bay and taking ferry rides to the Gulf Islands. After finding her an apartment on the outskirts of the City of Victoria it didn't take her long to settle in, make new friends, and find the location of the Catholic church.

Every Sunday, Elizabeth would come over to my house for a traditional roast lunch, beef or lamb, with all the trimmings. She loved my home-baked scones and fruit pies; I made sure she had enough goodies to take home with her. After lunch we would walk to my daughter's house close by and stop for tea. She loved my family and was especially tuned in to my three grandchildren—Christine, born in 1978, Robert, born in 1980 and Michael, born in 1987.

One day in early spring of 1991, after living three years in Canada, my sister was rather secretive on the telephone about something what she was about to tell me. I met her off the Victoria bus where it stopped at Robert's Bay and had Michael, a blond three-year-old grandson, holding my hand, to greet her. As we walked from the bus and headed toward my daughter's house, Elizabeth stopped halfway and said, 'I've something to tell you,' which I thought sounded rather ominous. 'Do I really want to hear what she is about to tell me?' I wondered.

'I've had a calling,' said my sister.

'What do you mean?' I asked, trying not to sound too concerned.

The response I received wasn't making sense, so I asked her to elaborate on what this "calling" was all about, but still made no headway in understanding what she was trying to convey to me. I sensed she did

Elizabeth, 30 years old, London, England.

not want to upset me and was finding it difficult to soften the blow with her surprising news.

Eventually arriving at the house I suggested that perhaps we have lunch first, and discuss what was on her mind later. After lunch we sat in the living-room and she gave me the news that she was returning to England to go into a convent at Rugby, way up the north of England. Her decision was like a hammer blow, shattering every nerve in my body. For a minute, I couldn't think, and sat glaring into the fireplace.

'Why?' I asked again.

Elizabeth replied, 'I've had a calling.' I still couldn't comprehend what she meant by a "calling," but then I realized she was convinced she was being called to serve God in a convent, somewhere out in the sticks at Rugby.

After being at a loss for words, I finally said, 'If that's what you want to do for the rest of your life I hope you will be happy, and the decision you have made is what you want.'

I then added, 'you know, we will all miss you.'

A few weeks later, saying goodbye to family and friends, Elizabeth flew back to Heathrow where she was met by our brothers Rowland and William. She stayed with William in Hampshire a few days, then met up with Rowland who bought her ticket to Rugby and saw her on the train to London. He said it broke his heart to see her go off alone, wondering what the future held for her.

We didn't have to wait long to receive news from the Mother Superior of the convent that my sister would have to come home as she was not strong enough to deal with her religious duties. Her religious duties, I was to learn later, included scrubbing red tiled floors. This information came from William, not Elizabeth. My brothers and I were devastated with the news. After the upheaval of selling her possessions and leaving a wonderful country like Canada, she was back living with William in Hampshire – her "calling" very much in question, and without a home.

This was not the first time Elizabeth had the desire to become a nun. At the age of twenty she was clothed with the Daughters of the Cross, who went around the district looking after the sick and dying. When I first visited her, after she entered the convent in Carshalton, Surrey, she appeared calm and happy wearing a novice's long, black dress. Once a month, relatives only were allowed a short visit, which took place in a tiny, cold room off the vestibule near the front door of the convent.

Noise of any kind was not permitted within the walls of the convent, neither were newspapers or radios. The nuns were not allowed conversation with one another and the only time a nun spoke, was when the Superior handed out instructions to her. This lack of communication within the convent, and the outside world, would later have a devastating effect on my sister who as long as I can remember, loved to chat and catch up with the latest world news. I wasn't impressed by these unnatural, at least to me, living conditions under which my sister now lived, and after saying goodbye to her at the front door of the convent, while on my way home, I mulled over her choice of lifestyle, and at the same time, was concerned for her health.

On my third visit to the convent I noticed Elizabeth was looking thinner and her countenance anything but happy. I was anxious about the pallor of her face, and had a strong urge to take her right out of the convent and back home with me. I realized of course this is not how she would want things done. Yet knowing her lack of physical strength was a risk, I felt it would only be a matter of time before she became aware that being a nun, however, desirable, was impossible due to her weak condition. As we sat in the tiny visitor's room I asked her if she was all right and needed me to bring anything with me next time I saw her, but she appeared vague and listless and said she was not allowed to accept material things. I was unable to extract any details of her new life and what duties she was expected to undertake, other than saying her daily rosary and prayers.

Once again returning home with a heavy heart, I wondered how long it would be before the convent realized my sister's health was deteriorating. It was less than a month since my last visit, when I received the Superior's letter telling me that Elizabeth was being sent home; no reason given. While I knew leaving the convent would be a great disappointment to my sister I tried to comfort her as best I could, telling her softly that although her desire to become a nun did not materialize, it did not necessarily mean she had failed God. She could still do good work by working with sick people in hospitals.

I must confess I was pleased with the convent's decision and knew that once I had my sister home, eating nourishing food and resting well, she would regain some of her lost weight and be back to her cheerful self.

Elizabeth on holidays in Lourdes, France, May 1981.

When this came about Elizabeth decided to train as a nurse, to care for the old and young, and did secure work in and around London. We met frequently and as she chatted, happily, about her work, I knew she had made the right decision. When staying with me over the week-ends, after going to our local church for Sunday mass, we returned home to cook a roast lunch, chat and relax.

On one occasion Elizabeth was asked by her church if she would help out in the priest's house. His housekeeper was recovering from an illness and had recently been discharged from hospital and wanted to spend Christmas with her family, who lived in the Surrey area. Always willing to help nurse the sick and dying, my sister agreed to undertake the housekeeper's duties over this period. She knew the priest as a quiet man, in his mid-forties, who suffered with diabetes. Once finding her bearings and seeing where everything was kept, she took care of the house and the priest's meals.

Knowing he was diabetic and his intake of sugar needed to be kept low, my sister decided to hide the tin of biscuits, normally kept within reach in the kitchen pantry. However, one afternoon when making his tea and looking for the biscuits, which she now gave to him one at a time, she was curious to find the tin half-empty. When she asked the priest about the missing biscuits, he told her he had eaten them.

'Father,' said Elizabeth, 'the sugar in the biscuits is bad for your health, but I'm sure it will be all right if you have just one a day.'

Laughing, chastising him at the same time, my sister asked the priest how he found the biscuit tin she had so carefully hidden.

'I knew where you had put it,' responded the priest.

After mass on Christmas day, Elizabeth set to preparing the turkey for the priest and three other priests whom he invited for dinner. All went well, the dining-room table was laid, until she took the turkey out of the oven and placed it from the roasting pan on to a serving platter. As she was about to enter the dining-room, the turkey slid off the platter and landed on the kitchen floor. Picking it up Elizabeth checked to see if any dust was on it and to make sure, used a damp paper towel to wipe the turkey breast. Assuring herself all was well, she put the turkey back on the platter and carried it into the dining-room to where the priest sat and placed it in front of him. While he sliced the meat, she fetched vegetables, gravy and trimmings from the kitchen to the table.

When Elizabeth told me this story, I envisaged the kitchen scene. Asking her how the priest liked his Christmas dinner, she gave me one of those innocent looks while smiling and said, 'Oh, he thoroughly enjoyed it, and so did his guests.'

I asked if she were unnerved by the incident. In true religious philosophy, she remarked, 'well, God saw the turkey fall off the platter and it was He who helped me put it back on.'

I could only hug her.

When I repeated her remark to Rowland, we laughed our heads off! 'Imagine,' I said to him, 'Elizabeth serving a turkey with God's help!'

Looking back, I am firmly convinced that the intensity of Elizabeth's religious beliefs were a result of extreme indoctrination during her childhood. Throughout her life, her convictions were unwavering, to the point these could never be diminished or erased. In her philosophy, however, she may have thought that she owed it to the church and God to give back what was given to her as a child, by becoming a nun. This is not a theory with which I can come to grips, despite all the reasoning in the church's teachings.

When Elizabeth left Canada she was beginning to look robust, happy, and enjoyed the life she had here with family and friends, socializing, going to theatres and concerts. When I flew back to Hampshire to visit her, I could have wept. She had lost considerable weight, looked fragile, and I was sure was worried what life now had in store for her since she was no longer wanted by the convent.

One evening, when staying with William, she decided to get on a chair in the kitchen to reach for food in a high cupboard, when she slipped and badly cut the back of her head. Blood poured all over the floor. William picked up Elizabeth, then telephoned for the ambulance that took her to Cosham Hospital, a few miles away from where he was living.

Upon receiving news of her accident I booked a flight to Heathrow and from there went immediately to the hospital to see her. For some reason the hospital had her in a room on her own but I did not question why. I asked the nurse at the station, close by, for the room number and when I saw Elizabeth and the state she was in, my heart went out to her. I noticed the front of her clothing was badly stained with food, also her left leg had enormous bruises on it.

I hugged her, then said, 'I'll be back.'

Like a mad bull, I dashed down to the nurses' station and demanded to see the person in charge. There was one girl at the front desk, busy chatting on the telephone, obviously to a boyfriend, so I banged on the counter and demanded, 'I want to speak with someone, now.'

'Oh, they're all busy,' the girl spoke, finally putting the receiver back on its cradle.

'You had better find me someone of authority, otherwise I have no choice but to create a disturbance.' Normally, a person of considerable tolerance, I did not want to use this threatening tone but knew if I didn't, I would get nowhere.

The girl could see I was not going to budge until I had some questions answered and called a person in charge, who was the manager. When I saw this man who appeared quite unconcerned with my concern, my mind went back to the days I lived in England when hospitals and patients alike were treated respectfully.

'What was needed here,' I thought, 'is a matron who walked the wards seeing everything was in apple-pie order, wearing a crisply starched uniform and a "puff" of a cap on her head, ensuring nurses and staff dealt efficiently with the work at hand, and that included the patients.'

After listening to my tirade, the manager arranged for two nurses to accompany me back to my sister's room. I first demanded to know why there were bruises on her leg. One nurse told me Elizabeth had fallen out of bed.

'Why then,' I asked, 'wasn't the side rails of the bed put up to avoid this happening?'

I got a blank look!

My next concern was her clothing so I insisted the nurse change those she had on, for clean ones. I told her my sister was not used to wearing dirty clothes, and that on my daily visits to the hospital I would be bringing in extra clothing. The nurse looked at me as though I'd gone raving mad!

Not satisfied, I went back to the nurses' station and spoke with the manager and told him I wanted to see my sister's doctor. He said he would phone and arrange an appointment for William and myself to see him.

On the appointed day I told the specialist of our concern about finding the condition my sister was in. Listening to me, he quietly said, 'You know, she is not very well, and now has the beginnings of Parkinson disease.'

This came as a shock to William and me, and my inner feeling was that perhaps this wasn't my sister's only health problem. We thanked the doctor for seeing us, but the information he gave about my sister's condition worried us, greatly.

Before we left his office he said, 'If there is anything further you wish to know, do not hesitate to call me.'

It was a few weeks later when the hospital rang to say they needed my sister's room and that we should find other accommodation for her as soon as possible, preferably a nursing home. William and I began searching the Southsea area, as this is where Elizabeth had spent some happy times; however, when checking out a few of the homes we were disgusted with what they had to offer a sick person. In fact, we were appalled at the condition of some of these nursing homes and one in particular called St. Patrick's was the worst of the bunch.

Ringing the doorbell at St. Patrick's we were escorted into the hallway, where we were met by the owner's partner. Wearing steel rings on both hands, chains, tight jeans, pink shirt, he had a cigar stuck in his mouth. I took one look at this gigolo and decided there and then my sister was not going to be dumped here. As we were inside the place my brother remarked, 'Well, now we're here, why don't we have a look around?'

Despite feeling reluctant, I nodded. As I envisaged, this would not be suitable accommodation for my sick sister, but agreed with his suggestion.

One look at the so-called bedroom, with no door, and being invited into the bathroom where a young girl was washing down an elderly lady, was enough for me. I turned tail and marched toward the front door, with William following close behind. I think the expression on my face told the proprietor the place was a disgrace. And to think they had the nerve to call it St. Patrick's.

After much searching the complete day in and around Southsea and feeling tired as well as frustrated, we decided to call it quits and go back

Back in England with Rowland, April 1991.

to William's home. Within days, fortunately, through a member of the church, William was told accommodation for Elizabeth was available in a nursing home at Horndean. Would we go and see it as soon as possible?

Wasting little time, arrangements were made for the ambulance to bring my sister from the hospital to the nursing home, where she would be looked after. William and I were delighted with this good piece of news as it was close to his home, and that meant he could visit her daily.

Her room was nicely furnished, and we noticed that the large window in it overlooked the gardens. 'Good,' I thought. Elizabeth loved flowers and this seemed an ideal place for her to look down on them. Once she settled into her new home we brought in additional items, floor rugs, a large armchair, and lots of colourful vases with flowers. We were anxious to make life for her as comfortable as possible, and I knew she appreciated everything we did.

The care she received at the nursing home in Horndean was second to none. The staff were attentive to everyone's needs and I must say I was impressed by the way the elderly were being taken care of. Any concerns or questions we put to them about Elizabeth's health were answered to our satisfaction. We were positive we had chosen the right place for her.

A few days after arriving at the nursing home it was Elizabeth's birthday, and one of the kitchen staff baked her a cake. We sat at the dining-room table. I saw her smile at the cake, then cut it into slices, put it onto a plate, and hand it to those sitting at the table. She took a small piece, but barely touched it. I sensed her health was deteriorating, and the thought saddened me.

The last day I saw my sister was when William and I popped in to see her, hoping she was comfortable and well. We chatted a while, then it was time for us to leave. I hugged Elizabeth and whispered, 'If I could take you back to Canada with me, I would.'

To which she weakly replied, 'I wish you would.'

From those words could I assume she was sorry to have left Canada, and that her "calling" had not materialized as she anticipated.

I didn't realize this would be our last conversation and that her life was slowly coming to an end.

I left England with a heavy heart, flying back to Canada. It would be only a matter of days before I received a phone call from William to say Elizabeth had taken a turn for the worse. By the time I had booked a flight and arrived back in Hampshire, my sister was dead. When William took me to see her coffin in the funeral parlour, I was upset to find the lid of the coffin had been firmly sealed.

'Why,' I asked my brother, 'did they have to seal the coffin without giving me a chance to see her, for the last time?'

Something he muttered made little sense. I felt I had been cheated of a final farewell, to a sister I dearly loved.

Attending a Requiem mass held at the Catholic church, with Rowland

and William standing on either side of me, with many of Elizabeth's friends from London and the church, I stared at the coffin in front of the altar over which was draped a white cloth, with tears flooding my face. After the service we walked slowly in procession, behind the priest, to the spot where my sister was to be buried. As I watched her coffin slowly descend into the ground, the realization that life can be snatched from you without warning, left me shivering with cold.

Elizabeth, my darling sister, now rests at Waterlooville, Hampshire. She was 64 years of age when she passed away July, 1993. The same age as our mother at her death. She had never married.

Ironically, in 1950 when Elizabeth and I spent time at Ramsgate with friends of hers, little did we realize our mother lived in Margate, a few miles away. One cannot begin to imagine what would have been said or done had we recognized her, and come face to face. The enormity of this meeting, no doubt, would have thrown us off balance. But fate, forever true, plays the ace card, with finality.

Elizabeth was the kind of person who saw good in everyone, rather than bad. If ever I complained about someone or something she would turn the discussion around to whomever I was speaking about, and give me the rundown on that person's positive attributes.

Her love of children was immense; it stressed her to see a child cry. When seeing any family members she fussed and fussed over them with obvious joy, and a big smile. She gave away freely her possessions, in the hope they would benefit someone else. A generous, loving, caring person, throughout her short life, she was a walking angel. We all miss her.

SOUTHSEA

After Elizabeth's funeral, Rowland decided to book bed and breakfast accommodation at Southsea, for a month. Perhaps this move by him was to get me away from the area where our sister's body was laid to rest, thinking that the salt sea air from the ocean breeze would do us both good.

Our accommodation was comfortable, and the breakfast provided was more than I could eat. Our host, an ex-naval man, and his wife ran the guest house and were extraordinarily kind to us. Rowland could not have picked a better place for us to stay. The shopping centre was within easy reach, and the seafront close by. We also found several small restaurants that served excellent dinners where we could sit at a quiet table, eat, and chat the evening away.

On one occasion we met up with a cousin who drove from Sussex to spend the day with us and stayed for dinner, before returning home. I don't know why, but Rowland decided we would celebrate Elizabeth's life with champagne. I wasn't sure if this was appropriate as I was still in shock from her death but I went along with the idea, while bubbles from the champagne foamed at my mouth. As it happened, it was an enjoyable dinner and we talked at length about the family, then our cousin said 'goodbye' and left. And we promised to write regularly to one another.

Southsea seafront has a spectacular panoramic views of The Solent and the Isle of Wight. Many years ago I remember going by ferry from Southsea to Shanklin, a small town on Isle of Wight. The ferries at that time were nothing more than cattle boats, with little room for sitting, so one stood most of the way. Fortunately, the trip across to Shanklin wasn't that long so one could tolerate standing the length of the journey, without putting too much strain on the leg muscles. Today the ferries are much more sleek, efficiently run, and obviously cater to the tourists.

The Castle at Southsea dates back to 1544 and was part of a series of fortifications constructed by Henry VIII around England's coasts to protect the country from invaders. Today it houses an exhibition on the military history of the town of Portsmouth. Rowland and I often popped into the exhibition to read up on historical documents, which were interesting. If one was caught in bad weather walking by the sea front, this was a great place to take cover on a rainy day and avoid being stung in the face by strong winds, prevalent along this coastline.

Each day we strolled along the promenade, taking in the sea breeze coming off the ocean and watched ferries going to and fro across the water. Often we sat on the castle's high concrete wall to watch high waves pounding the shoreline, over a pebbled beach, sometimes without saying a word – just looking, and perhaps in our minds thinking of those we recently lost.

I wasn't in any hurry to leave Southsea. Rowland made sure I had everything I needed and if we lunched, dined, or went by bus to Portsmouth or into other towns, he insisted on paying all expenses. I was overwhelmed by his generosity, and felt guilty about taking away necessities that could benefit his own family. But, he would have none of it when I mentioned this. At times I would become so emotional, I ended up crying.

'Don't cry,' he whispered, trying to stop the flow of tears, 'Elizabeth would not want you to be so unhappy.'

Several times, during our month's stay in Southsea, we hopped on buses to Portsmouth especially if we knew a football match was being played by the home team and one of the well-known away teams. The football field was a fair distance from town and after watching a game, we walked along to the Naval dockyard nearby. Rowland loved going into the dockyard and chatting to the officers, giving them snippets of his life in the Merchant Service which held their interest. It didn't matter to whom he was speaking, he was happier than a sand boy.

While the visiting public are allowed into the dockyard, with security men standing on guard at the gates, anyone wishing to visit a museum paid a small fee for this pleasure. One museum we greatly anticipated seeing was the *Mary Rose*; this proved a great disappointment, as all we saw were few pieces left of the ship. I wondered why all the effort and expense had gone into hauling these up from the ocean floor and put on display, whatever its historical connection. The *Mary Rose*, flagship of Henry VIII, built 1510, sank on July 19, 1545. What little remained of her was salvaged in October of 1982.

Commerce is noticeable when entering the dockyard. The gift shops display Naval maps, prints of ships on various fabrics, ship's bells, thimbles on which is imprinted the *Mary Rose*, chinaware, and many other pieces of Portmouth's history. While a portion of this revenue goes toward the preservation of the dockyard the commerce takes away from this once famous landmark and the history of men who served in large ships during the war. The silence and the cold atmosphere surrounding the dockyard gives a ghostly feeling of images past; as one looks around and notices the sadness of change, it's like looking into the soul of a deep grave. To see a naval dockyard such as Portsmouth, with few men and few ships in the harbour, leaves one with an incredible feeling of loss, wondering if all its past, priceless history was in vain.

We took lunch in one of the old Portsmouth pubs, whose pungent odour of beer, tobacco and timber hits the nostril upon entering. I marvelled how places this old, going back to Nelson's days, managed to stay afloat, with a good running business. The dining-room of the pub overlooked the harbour; a magnificent view, with the sun ablaze on the water, on this warm day. Ordering a luncheon of fresh sole, Rowland and I settled in to enjoy a cool drink while waiting to be served. When the meal was put before us although it looked appetizing, the food was not only cold, but the fish half-cooked. Rowland called the manager to complain. Picking up our plates the manger said he would ask the kitchen to serve us another. Second time round, the food was hot and well-cooked. A few minutes later the manager paused at our table, hoping he now had happy customers. We assured him, all was well. To compensate us he then said, 'dessert and coffee is complimentary.' While thanking him, he handed us his business card.

Looking at the name Marshall on it, we asked, 'any chance you could be related to us, with the same surname?'

'Hope not,' was his unexpected reply.

We looked at each other and laughed.

On a visit to Portsmouth we stopped by the terminal to check if there were ferries going to Cherbourg. Rowland wanted to revisit the port where his ship docked during World War II. In 1942, forces under the command of General Joe Collin's VII Corps cut off the Cherbourg Peninsula from the mainland, and seized the important fortress port from its German Commander. The Port of Cherbourg is at the Northern tip of the Cherbourg Peninsula, known in France as Haute Normande. It has a protected harbour with two long breakwaters. It is also a transatlantic seaport, a major naval base, and has a large marina.

Eager to see Cherbourg once more, Rowland booked our passages on the ferry. The following morning we were up at the crack of dawn, to be ready by six for our taxi to take us into Portsmouth in time to catch the eight o'clock ferry. The difference in furnishings on this ferry and comfort were remarkable, compared to the one I was on years ago to Shanklin, Isle of Wight.

Rowland, always a lover of food, suggested that as we had been up in the early hours and had no time even for a cup of tea, we go into the restaurant and have breakfast. As we entered the dining-room, the steward showed us a chair and once seated, handed us the menu.

Suddenly, I whispered to Rowland, 'I feel all wet.'

The surprised look on his face indicated he thought I was imagining things or making a joke.

'No,' I repeated, 'I'm all wet,' and stood up. Sure enough my slacks showed a wet patch, as a trickle of water ran down my legs.

Rowland called the steward to explain the situation. The steward was most apologetic and looked from me, to the chair, which I had now vacated. 'How,' I thought, 'am I going to dry off before landing at Cherbourg?' The answer was to wear my brother's coat and remove my slacks to be taken to dry out, somewhere on board. I wasn't sure if I appreciated eating breakfast in this fashion, but knew there was no other choice. The young steward could not apologize enough for the inconvenience; however, Rowland let it be known that incidents of this kind were unacceptable and should never happen if the dining-room chairs were checked after each sitting. Apparently a small child eating an earlier breakfast had caused the problem.

When we had finished breakfast and I was able to retrieve my slacks, now dried out, the young steward said we didn't have to pay the bill. Rowland wasn't exactly pleased with the morning's event, but we accepted his apology.

Throughout the journey we enjoyed the luxury of first-class seats in the lounge, where coffee was served. Rowland chatted away about his time during the war at Cherbourg, wondering if it had changed. All too soon it was time for us to leave the ferry and head for the town centre.

The Old Town is the main shopping area of Cherbourg. Here, in a maze of narrow cobbled streets, are packed specialist food and wine shops, cafés, bars and gift shops. Although it drizzled with rain, we made the best of our few hours before returning to the ferry. I don't think I have ever laughed so much with the way Rowland rushed me from place to place, post office to send off cards, liquor bar, the La Fayette store where he bought me lingerie by the dozen, and perfume that would last a lifetime.

Madame, at La Fayette, would throw lingerie of all kind, lacy, dainty, over the curtain rod, behind which I was furiously trying on one piece of flimsy at a time. I could hear Rowland laughing his head off in the background, prodding Madame along, to show me anything and everything he thought would suit me. By the time I had finished selecting different pieces of flimsies, we had the whole store in an uproar, wondering what these mad English people were all about. We left Madame shaking her head, but obviously pleased with the sales of the day.

Our next stop was the perfumery. The same performance. The salesgirls didn't quite know what to make of Rowland, who was asking for bottles of perfume and different nail polishes, which I didn't really need, and a grin so wide on his face, the girls started to laugh.

Looking at Rowland's face, so happy, I thought, 'What the heck, if he's enjoying it, so what! Let's go for broke.'

We came out of the store loaded with miniature bottles of perfume, plus two larger ones which he gave to me. One of my favourites was Clarins. With testing so many different sprays, we reeked of perfume. I couldn't begin to imagine what the wine shop proprietor would think of us, as we headed in his direction.

We entered the wine shop and if this didn't take the "cake," I don't know what did. Knowing Rowland did not drink I was somewhat surprised when he asked the French proprietor, in broken French, if he had any liquors? This lovely old man with a ginger beard and slight stoop went behind the counter and came up with several large bottles.

'Dear God,' I mumbled, 'I hope Rowland doesn't buy any of these, as we will never be able to carry them back to the ferry,' which was a good ten minutes walk from the town.

Not to be outdone, Rowland bought a large bottle of liquor brandy. I thought I'd die seeing him struggle with it, along with the rest of the shopping, still laughing his head off!

Although we had been up since the early hours of the day, on our return journey to Portsmouth, we had much to talk about, the places, people we met, and despite the drizzling rain, agreed we had had a "ball" of a day. With still a few days left before leaving Southsea we were determined to spend every hour together, walking, talking, making future plans for a life in Canada. It had the adrenaline flowing to a fast pitch.

Before leaving Southsea, Rowland told me he'd like to revisit Arundel Castle in West Sussex, the seat of the Duke of Norfolk, where he visited as a young boy. Never having been there, I thought it a good idea. Next morning we took an early coach from Southsea to Arundel, with the intention of spending the whole day looking around this historical town. The journey appeared never-ending but finally we arrived and got off the coach, which fortunately stopped right in the centre of the town.

As is normal with Rowland his first aim was to find the nearest place for lunch and this happened to be The King's Head, where they served excellent food. After lunch we ambled through the town and were heading toward a kiosk to pay our entry to the castle when suddenly a gypsy appeared and pushed a sprig of heather under my nose. I inched backwards, and told her I didn't want to buy it.

'Go away,' said Rowland to her sharply, pushing her from me, 'we don't want your heather.'

'Bad, bad luck, sir, if you don't buy,' was the gypsy's response.

As we walked away from the gypsy and reached the gates to the entrance of the castle I muttered to Rowland, 'I have visions of both our heads being chopped off.'

He roared laughing! 'Well,' he said, 'that being the case, we'll go down in history.'

Strolling toward the castle, I told Rowland of an incident with a friend of mine living in Bromley, Kent. About seven in the morning there was a knock on her front door and upon opening it, she came face to face with a gypsy who cried poverty and in the same tone told my friend if she bought the gypsy's flowers it would bring good luck. My friend who was hurriedly preparing to eat breakfast, then dash off to work, felt sorry for the gypsy so bought the flowers for the price of two shillings. Going into the kitchen she filled a vase of water and putting the flowers into it, suddenly realized they looked similar to the ones she grew in her garden.

Upon checking she discovered that, sure enough, the gypsy had stolen her flowers and sold them back to her!

Back in Southsea, we had much to talk about. The trip to the castle, with tombs of past dukes, and figures of ancient warriors wearing steel helmets and breast plates, standing rigidly in doorways, was impressive. I can only imagine the strength required when these warriors, heavily dressed, went into battle. Going down into the dungeon area, we entered a small tea-room, then stopped at the gift shop close by where replicas of historical scenes are imprinted on towels, china and other items of interest.

Whenever my mind goes back to that special day at Cherbourg where we laughed and ran in drizzled rain all over town, I look at the silver spoon he bought me there, hanging on my dining-room wall, and realize how lucky I was in finding Rowland, a man with a heart of sunshine, who found good in everyone, never stopped laughing, and chose to spend the rest of his life with his long-lost sister.

THE GARDENER

By 1992, Rowland was well and truly ensconced as a landed immigrant and we lived together in a house, in Sidney, B.C. A lover of gardening, he would spend hours outside looking after the lawns and flower beds. People passing by would stop to admire the garden and, of course, with an opportunity at hand, Rowland would chat and chat with them. His knowledge of plants, shrubs and trees was remarkable. He always knew the cause of canker or any other disease on plants and was reluctant to use herbicides on them, preferring a more natural solution to rid the plant of bugs.

Rowland was firmly convinced that shredded, unscented, household soap, mixed with water and sprayed on roses, destroyed aphids that inhibited the growth of the plant. This solution not only protected the new buds but helped prevent black spot from spreading on the leaves.

A week never went by when Rowland didn't cut fresh flowers from the garden and put them in the living-room on the coffee table. He disliked putting white lilies, or any other white flowers with red ones in a pot, as they were a constant reminder these were the colours used at funerals. Often, I watched him, balanced on a shovel, chatting away to his heart's content to a neighbour outside. He loved people and talking to anyone who had the time of day to listen to him. Forever being questioned about gardens he was only too pleased to give every detail on how to go about looking after them to anyone interested.

He potted up with flowers two large Grecian urns which he stood on the front doorstep outside the house; the plants were of every colour, and as the trailers grew they cascaded over the urns. I was forever enthralled when he planted these up with new soil and seasonal plants, as they were done to perfection. The admiration on Rowland's artwork received from people passing never ceased to amaze me and had me feeling as proud as punch.

We also grew bushels of vegetables in the garden and with the abundance of peas and beans I was able to freeze many of them for us to enjoy in the winter months. The apple and pear trees and blackcurrants supplied us with so much fruit that we often left baskets on the front lawn, for people to help themselves. Many times a smile would appear on our faces as we watched from the living-room window as passersby helped themselves to fruit off the trees near the sidewalk, without the courtesy of a knock on the front door for permission. Knowing they would enjoy the fruit, we had no qualms when they simply helped themselves to whatever they needed from either pear or apple tree.

Sometimes when I called him in for coffee at mid-morning, Rowland was nowhere to be found. Minutes later, as he arrived back at the house, I would say, 'Been for a walk?'

To which he would reply, 'I went down the road with a lady who needed advice on her garden.'

'Nice of you,' I said, giving him a saucy smile.

When I remarked how lovely the garden always looked, with the lawns well-cut, and his endless knowledge of plants, he surprised me one day by saying that when he worked in his father-in-law's greenhouses in England, he didn't know a weed from a flower. I found this rather hard to believe, but he assured me this was so. I was to learn that sixty years after he worked in the greenhouses, that experience would determine the cause of his death.

Although Rowland worked full time at the Mersey Docks and

Harbour Board in Liverpool as a Marine Supervisor, in his off-duty hours he trudged over to the greenhouses where Stan, his brother-in-law, worked alone to give him a helping hand. Despite the long hours he put in, his father-in-law, a miserable miser of a man, never offered to pay him one cent. Rowland neither expected it, nor wanted it, but said the offer would have been appreciated.

Stan was a gentle, conscientious man who kept the greenhouses up and running so that his father could have the benefit of his hard work. However, whatever he did, and no matter how hard he worked, it was never enough for the old man. Although he expected Rowland to deliver the goods like Stan, the old man was aware that if he demanded too much of him, knowing his job at the Harbour Board paid well, Rowland would probably have thrown the shovel at him and left. But, for Stan's sake, he kept the peace.

One day, Rowland spotted a stray cat in the greenhouses and it was obvious to him that this animal knew its way around the potted plants. There were also signs of nesting material on the concrete floor, which appeared to come from the warm pipes, above. As Rowland called Stan to tell him about the animal, the cat fled out of the open door and disappeared. Stan said he had seen this cat before, and knew it had been getting into the bird's nests and killing the young ones.

'Right,' said Stan, 'next time it comes in, I'll show it where it belongs.'

It wasn't long before the cat decided to take a chance and ambled, nonchalantly, inside the greenhouses. But Stan was there waiting and, within seconds, grabbed the cat and threw it bodily into his rabbit's cage, just outside the door. All hell broke loose as the rabbit, an angora, thumped the cat with its feet which, by now, was shrieking murder, with fur flying everywhere. Rowland and Stan stood outside watching the performance and after one or two minutes when Stan thought, enough was enough, he opened the cage door of the rabbit's hutch and the cat fled, as though on fire. Needless to say, it never returned.

A weekly event at the greenhouses was when a certain local wealthy lady came to pick up her regular order of flowers. Fastidious, to the point of idiocy, she examined every bloom offered and if there happened to be a slight kink in a stem or what might have looked like a flower lost one petal, she demanded new ones.

This particular lady was the wife of an Army Colonel and I'm sure she thought herself, "the cat's whiskers." She was never without her pooch; the dog would walk down to the bottom of the road, sniffing all the way, and ultimately end up meeting Rags, a large grey scruffy dog that belonged to a neighbour. After preliminary greetings with one another, Rags would lift his leg and politely spray the pooch with urine.

When the dog finally trotted back up to the greenhouses, the owner would run to pick it up, snuggling the pooch in her arms and kissing the dog all over. Rowland and Stan watched this performance many times and chuckled to themselves, knowing the habits of Rags and how he left his calling card on any dog that trespassed on his territory.

Often the old man miser would come up to the greenhouses to pick up money from the sales of flowers and certain vegetables which they grew along with many varieties of plants. He would inspect the garbage pile round the back of the greenhouses, sort out the "spoils" thrown into it, clean and dust them off, then put them for sale in customer's orders. Rowland said that sometimes the tomatoes he picked off the pile were beyond human consumption, but the old man would have none of it, if either Stan or Rowland made any comment. He would snarl at them, saying, 'it's none of your business.'

The men looked at each other thinking that some unsuspecting bugger will get Montezuma's revenge.

When the outside covers of the greenhouse boilers needed to be upgraded Stan and Rowland would get barrels of asbestos powder, scoop some out into a large bucket, then mix it with water into a paste. Once they had the right consistency the men would pick up another bucket, fill it, and with their hands apply the paste around the boilers, making sure it was well sealed. When the asbestos paste dried, it provided excellent insulation cover for the boilers. Doing repairs of this type on many jobs in the greenhouses saved the old man hundreds of pounds sterling.

It was Rowland's contention that using asbestos, a deadly chemical, in the greenhouses caused Stan's early death. He died of cancer at forty-three years of age.

Although it took sixty years for the asbestos to show up in Rowland's case. He did not discuss the matter with me until the doctors determined this was the cause of his health problem. Several doctors in the Victoria hospitals did many tests on him but were unable to pinpoint the reason for his illness. It wasn't until all avenues had been explored that the doctors became aware he had a condition known as congestive heart failure, causing the lungs to fill up with fluid that required periodical draining. When they discovered Rowland used asbestos some years ago, their analysis was decisive.

It was the old miser's legacy.

DELIRIOUS TIMES

That's exactly what they were! Deliriously happy times with children as tiny as six months old.

Putting the work force behind me in Ontario, I couldn't wait to retire in my new home here in British Columbia and sit back, leisurely, doing my own thing, reading, writing, gardening and baking oodles of pies, cakes and scones. If anyone told me I would be looking after children as young as six months old, I probably would have looked hard at them in disbelief.

Although long retired Rowland and I were eager to accept the offer made by a Beacon Community councillor, whom we grew to love, to look after children between the ages of six months to four years old at the Mothers & Babies group, held each Wednesday between ten o'clock and twelve noon at St. Paul's United church in Sidney.

We both adored children, especially the underprivileged ones, and went into the programme with great energy. What we experienced with these small children was not only the joy they gave us, which came totally unexpected, but the effect it had on our lives would remain with us, forever.

The Mothers & Babies programme was initially set up by the Beacon Community to allow mothers quality time off, away from the young ones.

Their meeting room was next door to where the children were looked after, and weekly speakers came in to advise them on dental and general welfare of young children. It also gave them an opportunity of meeting other mothers in the same community, as well as socializing with them over cookies and coffee.

We did not anticipate looking after children as tiny as six months when we agreed to undertake the programme and were immensely surprised, one day, to be handed a six-month-old baby boy to look after. The distressed mother didn't know how to pacify him as the little fellow was crying blue murder, so I asked her to give him to Rowland. Never having met either one of us before, we assured the mother he will be well taken care of and if she was still in doubt, she could come in any time to pick him up. The mother said the baby's name was Zachary and handed the boy into Rowland's arms, and left to go to the mothers gathering next door.

With the child in his arms Rowland cooed and nursed the infant and before long the young boy was sleeping soundly. Having stopped the crying and knowing the young child was relaxed, Rowland then placed the baby in a cot with lots of soft blankets and kept an eye on him, while settling down to play with the other children. Over the months, as we watched Zachary grow into a handsome blond, blue eyed boy, we noticed his gentle disposition and a smile so big it would melt an iceberg. When he began walking and came into the playroom carrying his favourite toy, he ran towards Rowland who picked him up and gave him big hugs. This child who gave love so freely, at times, overwhelmed us. Always cheerful, I can never remember seeing him cry, or wanting a toy held possessively by another child. Like all children, he was very special.

Normally, there were about six or seven children in our group, ranging from months old to four years in ages, but sometimes one or two more children would creep in, on the odd occasion. Although we had no desire to be too regimental with the children we realized if we were all going to have fun together there needed to be some organization at hand, to maintain the children's interest and keep them happy.

Zachary at 28 months, 1996.

The big toy box, heavily-filled, would be dragged out of the playroom cupboard, with the children helping, and around a small table they would sit on tiny chairs and we would have fun brick-building, which was always a favourite, along with book colouring. There was, however, one little rascal who couldn't wait for the house of bricks to be built and before any of us could sit back and admire it, he would send it crashing to the floor.

The oos and aahs that came from the children indicated disappointment because they were unable to admire this work of art which everyone had helped to create, due to one little boy's determination to smash it to pieces. We would discover, later, there were problems within the family and in his anger the boy wanted to destroy anything and everything that came his way.

Rowland and I developed a special attachment to this four-year-old child and while in our company showered him with love and kindness, which we hoped would remain with him when times were difficult throughout his life. Eventually, he came to put his trust in us and the minute Rowland entered the room the child took precedence, sitting on my brother's lap before any other child could get near it. When asked by our lady counsellor if we would sit once or twice in his home, we agreed, but that's another story.

At eleven o'clock we stopped for snacks and juices provided by Beacon Community, who were generous with variety and quantity. Sitting the children around the small table we offered a plastic plate with cheese, crackers in the shape of fish or animals which the children loved, fruit and juice, ensuring each child had his or her fair share and whatever food was left over we passed around.

One delightful four-year-old, chubby red-head, whom I will christen Mandy, always beautifully dressed, had a yen for cheddar cheese and couldn't get enough of it. If there happened to be the last piece left on the plate, she considered it to be hers. With chubby fingers, she would try to overpass Rowland's hand to grab the last cube of cheese from the serving plate. In a softly-spoken voice Rowland explained to her that the other children might also like the last piece but if they didn't, she could have it.

'We must share, mustn't we?' he said to our red-head.

I'm not sure if he entirely got the message across. She kept him to his word and never failed to remind him of his promise, to give her the last piece of cheese.

Mandy was a child who loved hugging and kissing. Often we watched her with arms tightly-held round the neck of another child, perhaps younger than her, pecking the child on the cheek. This was a beautiful gesture, and we had no intention of preventing her display of exuberant love for another. However, the child who was on the receiving end of all this love would struggle to remove Mandy's arms – perhaps feeling a little frightened that something untoward might happen. In so doing, the smaller child of the two would suddenly stagger and if not caught in time, would fall on the floor. Watching carefully to avoid mishaps, Rowland and I would diligently watch Mandy out of the corner of our eye, to ensure accidents did not happen and that the children were not hurt.

One day Mandy did get a bit overzealous with affection. We had to quietly take her arms from around the neck of another child and explain to her that loving was one thing, but the recipient was not in favour of being half-smothered. From that day on, Mandy would peck a child on the cheek, she didn't mind if it was boy or girl, and happily kiss us the same way.

When we mentioned to her mother how much affection and love Mandy had to give, her response was, 'Yes, she simply loves kissing and hugging.'

Years later, when we no longer looked after children, Rowland and I met Mandy and her mother in town. Mandy had grown into a red-head beauty!

After snack-time we would sing, play games of hide and seek, while keeping an eye on babies in the cots, and a favourite – "ring around the roses." How Rowland and I ever managed to get up off the floor amazes me to this day, but we did, after we all fell down.

Often when looking up at the door, where passersby could see through a window the goings-on inside, we spotted one or two mothers who perhaps had visited the ladies room, smiling, to watch the children playing and singing.

Half an hour before leaving, we had clean-up and "dribble the ball" time. Rowland never could forget the fun he had when playing football as a youngster, and showed the children how to kick the medium-size soft ball and dribble it toward a four-year-old goal keeper. I wished I'd had a camera at this point, as watching tiny feet struggling to keep command of the ball and falling over themselves, was like watching a Charlie Chaplin movie. Rowland and I would double up with laughter, with little faces watching us, curiously, wondering what it was all about.

Again, our little rascal thought he would take "the field" and bash the ball hard up against the back wall of the room, closely missing the windows.

Taking him aside Rowland whispered, 'Should you break the windows, it could injure one of the children or babies. That would hurt, and make them sad. You wouldn't want that to happen, would you?'

Instead of being contrite, our rascal gave Rowland a cheeky grin.

When it was time to leave, several of the children didn't want to go home, despite persistent wrangling from the mother that the playroom was now closed. Rowland would step in and quietly persuade the child it was home time, and that we also had to leave.

'We'll have as much fun next week, won't we?' he said, holding onto a small hand to get the child out of the door. 'What's more,' he added, 'we will sing, and dribble the ball.'

While we didn't love one child more than the other, there was a two-year-old who insisted on calling us "Mama and Papa." She came from a large family and had the most caring of mothers. If Rowland and I were in town shopping and this little angel spotted us, she would come running with hugs and kisses, calling, 'Mama, Papa,' as though we were manna from heaven. We returned the affection, overjoyed that such emotion could come from one so young. We realized there are no boundaries when children love, freely, if you are willing to accept it. Once they reward you with their implicit trust, they are never judgemental of your actions. This feeling of love was mutually shared, and treasured, by young and old.

After many, many months of child-caring at the Mothers & Babies group we were asked by our same counsellor if we would be willing to take another group held at a clinic, near the local hospital. This programme would be run on the same lines as that of the morning group on a Wednesday, but the time ran from one o'clock to three.

Rowland and I did not hesitate to accept another challenge, with different mothers and children, when this offer was made, despite the fact that we were aging and wondered if we had the strength to lift a child, or play "dribble the ball."

Before leaving the house in the morning I would pack a lunch so that we could eat before going on to the second group of mothers and children. Having one hour to relax, eat, and enjoy the scenery at Lockside, conversation usually centered around the events of the mornings and the fun we had had with the children. What made it all the more special was that our counsellor seemed pleased with our work and it appeared that comments were made to her about us by the children's mothers who, obviously, were also pleased with the way we handled their children. It was a recommendation, indeed, for us to feel we were doing a splendid job, giving tender, loving care to the young.

Although we enjoyed most of the children's groups we had a special interest in the Wednesday morning sessions at St. Paul's United church as the facilities offered were superior to any of the others. Being closer to home was another factor. We met many mothers who asked us to baby-sit in their homes and were delighted to help out, time-permitting.

One such family living in the Deep Cove area asked me if I would baby-sit two small children once or twice a week, depending on the mother's needs, to shop or simply take a break from the house. I noticed the mother was heavily pregnant and realized her request for help with the children made it that more special.

Fortunately I was still driving but to reach the house, which stood at the top of a long driveway, it meant I had to cautiously drive the car up a steep slope to get to the property. This was fine during the warmer months but when winter arrived every nerve in my body was strung taut, like guitar strings, when I drove on ice and snow, making it treacherous for me to drive. When the weather turned bad and I decided it wasn't worth the risk, I was forced to leave the car at the bottom of the road and walk up a slippery, icy driveway, holding onto shrubs and bushes as I reached the top.

I stayed with this lovely family for many months and if anyone should be accredited for their welfare and upbringing, it is their mother. I loved her style, she was direct and to the point with all three children and if eye contact was denied her, she would softly say, 'Please, look at me.' What a learning experience for these children, who are now in their young adult years, to be given the opportunity of knowing how to communicate with one another because of an understanding, caring mother.

When her second son was born, Rowland on many occasions came with me to the house. As he watched with anticipation the mother and baby together, I knew he couldn't wait to touch and hold the child. Quietly watching him out of one eye I could see him waiting with bated breath for the mother to hand over her son. When the baby was in his arms he would croon, hug and nurse him and when looking down at him, offered a smile as wide as an ocean. As this little boy grew up, with his shy disposition, he displayed an irresistible charm that gave us the urge to want to take him home, but we knew his family would love him deeply for all time and give him the nurturing he needed.

Memories of this young family are indicative of what family life is all about. How we loved spending time with them. And later, receiving an annual Christmas photograph of the family, showing how the children have grown up, and news of their achievements throughout the year.

When spending time at the two mothers groups, we tried not to play favourites with one child from the other as, to us, they were all special human beings, each with their own personality, more enduring than the next.

There was, however, a two-year-old boy who truly pulled the strings at my heart, in many ways. When I first met him, at a different group, he was reticent, shy, and would not "open up" to encouragement from either Rowland or myself. How to win him over would take years but when you earned his trust he became the most loveable, intelligent young boy, with curly hair and large brown eyes.

One day I was asked by his mother if I would babysit him, while she and her husband went for a twenty-minute coffee break. I was more than happy to oblige, knowing they both needed a little time to themselves. On the appointed day I arrived early at their home and did this intentionally in order to acquaint myself with James. Going over one or two items with his mother, covering unexpected emergencies, she told me where she left his afternoon snack and, if necessary, extra clothing that might be needed. The parents then left.

The minute the front door closed behind them James, with his arms spread-eagled across the frame of the door, began bawling his heart out. Left with a sitter for the first time he cried and cried so much, he eventually ended throwing up. I had been sitting on the floor sorting out his toys and trains, along with many other items made of soft material or wood, and hoped to gain his interest, with no result. I went over to him. As I approached him and he pushed me aside, I spoke gently while persuading him to come with me into the bathroom so that I could clean him up and if necessary, put a clean shirt on him. Having done that, I proceeded to mop up the living-room floor, then asked James if he would like his snack. The response was negative. His one aim was to cling with arms spread-eagled across the front door, until his parents returned, and bawl his head off.

Hardly having been away for twenty minutes the parents returned, asking questions of how it went while they were gone. I gave them a brief run-down of what happened, then left to return home. A few days later I received another phone call, asking if I would baby-sit James again. When I arrived I approached the child, gently speaking to him, then chatted to his parents with the assurance – all will be well, go have a coffee, and enjoy a good half-hour together.

As was my usual tactic to get James's attention, I tipped the toy box in the living-room and began sorting and building bricks, at the same time keeping an eye on the boy, hoping we might communicate. I tried not to notice him and he in turn would give me a look with his large brown eyes.

'Who's playing this cat and mouse game?' I wondered. But I wasn't prepared to back down.

After his parents left I envisaged another performance of him holding onto the front door, bawling, with arms spread-eagled, but this did not happen. Some minutes later, after wandering around the living-room, he decided to check on what I was doing with his toy box and without further ado, sat down on my lap. I picked up some bricks and started building with them. To keep his interest going I then opened a book and with a variety of pencils began to colour, but he took the pencil from my hand as he wanted to do the picture himself.

To my utter amazement, James then began chatting quietly, showing me his toys, and his favourite one. At last, we were making progress. I was beginning to feel great with anticipation that perhaps, eventually, he would put his trust in me. When his parents returned from having coffee I assured them James and I had had a good time while they were gone, and that he did not cry or hang onto the door when they left. He was also a good boy to eat his snack.

There were no further outbursts of wanting Mummy and Daddy. In fact, when they decided to go out for a longer period of time, young James would see them off with a 'goodbye' then promptly return to me, sitting on the floor, and the games and fun would begin. We had developed a trusting relationship.

At a young age James knew exactly the path he would follow in his adult years and told me many times that the dollars saved in his money box would be solely used to further his education when attending university. He was a remarkable young man, highly intelligent for his age, and with a vision and determination to not stray from his chosen path until he achieved his goal. When hearing of his dreams, my admiration for him hit the heights! The last time I saw James was in 2007 at a ceremony held at University of Victoria, where Parkland high school students were presented with diplomas and caps, having graduated with top marks.

When Rowland and I finally decided the time had come to give up child-minding, we knew we would miss them. Not only were they our friends who gave so much love, and fun, but they trusted us implicitly. Our relationship with them was second to none.

TRIPS GALORE

Now that Rowland and I had free time on our hands, we went on frequent ferry trips either to Vancouver or the Gulf Islands. Whenever an opportunity presented itself, I would urge Rowland to come with me and he seldom refused. However, if I suggested going on an ocean cruise, which I'd never been on, he would say, 'I've been on so many ships throughout my life in the Merchant Navy and the idea of getting on another one doesn't appeal to me.'

'So,' I thought, 'that was that!' Although I appreciated the way he felt about getting on another ship, I knew pressuring him to change his mind would be futile, even for me, whom I knew he loved. However the urge to go on a cruise did not prevent me from thinking that perhaps, one day, this would become a reality.

A pattern emerged: taking the car to Swartz Bay, a short distance from the house, we left it in the short-term parking lot and walked toward the ticket area where we were handed our boarding passes for the ferry we chose to go on that day. Between Mondays and Thursdays seniors are allowed to use the ferries without charge so we took advantage of these days to go on as many trips possible. It didn't really matter which ferry we chose but if it was one going to Vancouver we checked the weather forecast and if good, knew we would enjoy a warm, sunny day, sitting out on deck, while taking benefit of an invigorating breeze off the ocean. Once boarded we leisurely lunched in the buffet lounge, at the same time seeking out wildlife. Occasionally, we might spot the odd seal or two and many sea birds diving and feeding round Active Pass, but eagle or whale sighting was rare.

The Vancouver ferry leaves Swartz Bay every other hour. The early morning ferry is usually brimming with people who work in the City, and sit reading their newspapers and perhaps catching up with the latest financial news. Passengers who take daily trips, like us, generally enjoy being out on deck, taking in the ozone, and watching the sun dazzle the water on what looks like sparkling diamonds, as we drift by.

These were truly great trips to Vancouver and back, and Rowland and I revelled in the relaxed atmosphere. If we had any worries these were immediately thrown overboard, carelessly to the wind, hoping the Gods would take care of them.

After lunch we browsed around the gift shop and, as usual, Rowland would ask if there was anything I wanted. It was seldom anything took my eye so, politely, I would refuse his offer. Apart from that, knowing he was on a fixed pension, I preferred he spent money on himself, rather than on me. But, as always, he looked after my interest first, which was overwhelming!

When the ferry docked near Vancouver we stayed on board and obtained a return ticket from the gift shop, so that we were counted for when the ferry headed back to Swartz Bay, one and a half-hours later.

We took many trips to the Gulf Islands, visiting Mayne, Pender, Otter Bay, Village Bay, where the ferry docked to drop off and pick up passengers at each island. We were thrilled to spot more wildlife in these areas, eagles in particular, soaring in and out of the thermals. The *M.V. Cumberland* ferry to these islands leaves Swartz Bay at 10.20 a.m., returning nearly three hours later, at one o'clock. It was a great way to pass the time of day looking at the scenic mountains, and catching sight of soaring eagles.

On one of our many trips. Vancouver, BC is in the background.

Salt Spring Island is one of the Gulf Islands in the Strait of Georgia located between mainland British Columbia and Vancouver Island, and the most populated of the Islands. In 2008, the census recorded 10,500 residents.

We always enjoyed our visits to Salt Spring, not only because we were able to take the car, but being the largest of the Islands, it is an interesting place for shopping. Its history of European settlers dates back to the 1800s. Before 1871 all settlers intending to acquire land through "pre-emption" could occupy and improve the land before purchase. They were permitted to buy it at a cost of one dollar per acre after proving the work was done.

During the 1960s the island became a refuge for US citizens dodging the draft during the Vietnam War, much to the concern of some local inhabitants.

The ferry crossing from Swartz Bay to Salt Spring is smaller than those going to the other Gulf Islands. This ferry takes thirty-five minutes from Swartz Bay. When the ferry docked at Fulford Harbour we drove into the town of Ganges and spent the day browsing, lunching and enjoying the scenery. On our return journey we were sure to be back at Fulford Harbour, in time for the 6 p.m. crossing.

Salt Spring Island is noted for breeding sheep; its spring lamb is available to those visitors wishing to buy it. The first time I bought a leg of Salt Spring lamb I found the flavour much stronger than the New Zealand lamb which I bought frequently when living in England. The New Zealand lamb is less pungent and cooked slowly retains the delectable juices, making the meat very tender. With mint sauce and new potatoes, there is no other dish to beat it.

The Saturday market at Salt Spring is worth a visit, as there is plenty to catch the imagination. Jostling with the crowds makes it, if not a tiring day, an interesting one. Among other produce available locally, there is a wide variety of freshly-baked breads and confectionery to be had, and delectable cheeses, plus local artisan jewellery and clothing. Some of the artwork's vibrant colours, and up-to-date styles in clothing, are solely for the attraction of young people. Not quite my cup of tea!

Ganges, the largest town on Salt Spring, has always been known as an arty place. Notable also are the "hippies" who seem to drift on and off the island, perhaps searching for some inner peace and simple lifestyle. Work being difficult to find, one assumes most are on government support. Analyzing the situation I could only conclude this is where these people chose to be, without having to endure the everyday stresses of urban living, trying to make ends meet, and enjoy what surely is nothing short of paradise on Salt Spring Island. To them, as with many visitors, the tranquility of the island gives one a feeling of inner peace.

Rather than drink the ferry's strong coffee I would bring a thermos with me, along with a freshly-baked muffin. This was specifically for Rowland's benefit rather than mine, as he wasn't a coffee-drinker, and the weaker it was the better he liked it. When taking these trips we also brought along an English newspaper and once settled in our appointed seat would look at the crossword puzzle, tackle anagrams and other clues, while chatting and enjoying the scenery. I can't remember on any trip finishing the crossword!

On one of these trips I was to discover a quirky side of Rowland's character that had me shaking my head when it first happened. I wasn't to realize, then, this would not be just the odd occasion; there would be numerous ones to come, which never failed to surprise me. We would be settled nicely on a front seat in the lounge, facing the bow of the ship, when suddenly he would disappear. Thinking he may have gone to the little boy's room I kept myself busy doing the crossword puzzle but after a lengthy period became a little anxious, and had visions of him going over the side of the ship. Then I thought, 'He can't be that daft to go overboard.'

When he finally emerged and came back to his seat, I asked, 'Are you all right?'

'Oh yes,' he replied, 'just chatted to a fellow a few seats down, who was extremely interested in some of the yarns I told him of my adventures in the Merchant Navy.'

Listening to the stories he related to me, over many months, about his career in the Service, I enticed him to put the details down on paper and write a book. When he completed his autobiography, recording his experiences at home and abroad, I read the draft proof and found it incredible that after many years past, he was able to remember small details of his career. Outlining the historical events, plus his command of accents in different languages, which is a writer's nightmare unless thoroughly conversant with foreign tongues, not only amazed me, but I found remarkable.

Rather than drive the car into Victoria, to avoid parking problems, we took the bus from Sidney. Once aboard the bus, which was normally filled with people coming off the ferry from Swartz Bay, we settled into a seat while watching the scenery go by, and people getting on and off the vehicle. Suddenly, I would turn my head to where Rowland was sitting, only to find his seat, vacant.

The first time this happened I thought he had jumped off at a stop, without saying a word. As usual, I wondered what happened to him, when looking around the bus searching for faces, he could be seen jawing "ten to the dozen" to a group of young people sitting at the back of the bus. As long as I knew he was safe I didn't take much notice and when he came back to his seat, grinning like a Cheshire cat, I almost fell off my seat, laughing.

'At it again,' I teased, without chastising him, useless it would have been if I wanted to, adding, 'and did you have a good chat?'

I then asked Rowland that when he decides to do the disappearing act on me, to let me know, so that I didn't have to worry about his safety. I received a positive response from him but knew on future trips into Victoria and ferry rides to the Islands he would be as impulsive as ever, and go his own way. I wasn't wrong. He reminded me of a lightweight boxer whose feet never stopped moving.

Victoria had a beckoning affect on us. We loved the inner harbour, watching float planes coming and going past Laurel Point, as well as chatting to various artists painting vibrant coloured artwork on the concrete slabs. The Royal B.C. Museum was another attraction where we would spend hours going from floor to floor looking at exhibits of extinct birds and animals. The Woolly Mammoth, a large prehistoric elephant, takes pride of place as one enters the exhibits. Sometimes we would amble along to the tiny pioneer-era cinema, on the upper floor, and watch an old Charlie Chaplin movie and roar our heads off. It was a great place to sit, relax and have a jolly good laugh.

At Victoria's main downtown mall, which was then the Eaton's Centre, we would lunch first. Rowland's craving for food was incredible.

Although slimly-built, he had an appetite second to none. I often wondered where he put all the food he ate, as I definitely could not at any time keep up with him. But, he enjoyed eating, and who was I to deny him that pleasure, despite some days I did not feel like eating at all.

After lunch we browsed through Eaton's and as we approached the cosmetics department, he would stop at the Clarins counter and say to me, 'Do you need any more make-up?' Knowing Clarins was my favourite, he would get the adrenaline flowing to such a pitch not only to me, but the sales girls, whom he had scurrying under the counter for the latest samples of face and hand creams, to give to me.

Rowland picked up items of cosmetics he knew I used, but before I had the chance to say anything he would hand me the jar – 'Yes, you need this, and yes, you mentioned wanting a different colour lipstick, so while we are here, have a new one.'

By the time he had finished buying, the cost of make-up added to over three hundred dollars! I was shocked in embarrassment. I could only thank him for his generosity but hope the next time we went into Eaton's, we could avoid the cosmetics counter.

One of Rowland's favourite sayings, which I heard repeatedly from him, was that he didn't want to be the richest man in the cemetery. I thought, 'My darling, if you continue going on spending sprees like this, for whomever's benefit, your wish will certainly be granted.'

As we progressed visiting other stores in the mall, Rowland would usually wait for me, but occasionally I found I was speaking to myself, as he had done another disappearing act. This was more serious than being on the ferry or bus because without a word he was gone, but where, I had no idea. Suddenly, he would resurface to my side grinning from ear to ear which, initially, I found funny. However, when it happened a few times, I reasoned, this has to stop.

My shopping plan with Rowland was that if he decided to do the disappearing act and strike up a conversation with passersby about his naval experiences, I would wait for him on the upper floor, and sit in one of the armchairs. Other than that I would meet him outside the mall, where we caught the bus back home. This worked considerably well. I explained to him that I had no intention of restricting his movements but it concerned me when he decided to wander off, and I thought it best we returned safely home together, to which he agreed.

HERBAL MADNESS

It was my firm conviction that when one baked breads, and the like, various spices were used to enhance the flavour. When preparing a dish of meat or fish, one recognized that palatable cuisine required the use of many good herbs to whet the appetite and increase the taste buds. Selecting those that included antitoxins assured me that what we were eating was for the good of our health.

Throughout my years as a young housewife, the only known herbs were those grown in our garden of parsley, sage and thyme. This lack of knowledge of other herbs came about due to strict regulations during World War Two when seeds were unavailable to put in the garden, or allotment, despite increased publicity for the people to grow vegetables for victory. Knowledge of herbs, therefore, did not come into play until many years after the war. Sometimes, to get a little more variety of vegetables or herbs, one scrounged from friends and neighbours. The camaraderie between people throughout the war and post-war years was truly remarkable. With everyone living under the same strict conditions it was evident help of any kind would be accepted, and appreciated.

Over the years, due to much advertising, the public have come to realize the benefits of herbs and spices and today there are more health food stores than one can count, selling these supplies. Experience using herbal medicine for health problems has convinced a large section of the populace that these have less damaging effect on the body than pharmaceutical drugs; while at the other end of the scale, doctors do not recommend them to patients because many of the herbal concoctions have not been scientifically proven. Despite this, more and more people use herbs, lotions and teas to the extent it has become a viable market.

Often Rowland would check the Internet to find out what herb cured a specific ailment. Sheets and sheets of information coming off the printer, recommending this or that herb, would leave me in doubt. While I wanted to be supportive, I did not wish to take all I had read from the Internet as gospel but, of course, my dear brother was ready to believe and try anything. You could not convince him otherwise.

His implicit faith in herbal medicines was getting to the point of paranoia, to which I could not keep pace with the different types he sampled and bought home. With every new ache or pain, like a young boy on his new scooter, he would charge into town and head directly to the health food store, convincing the sales lady what he was buying would cure a certain ailment. As usual when shopping, which was a constant merry-go-round, the sales lady and customers alike would listen to his chatter how certain herbs worked for him. However, he did not pay much attention to the idea that some herbs that suited his ailment did not necessarily agree with others, regardless of whether they suffered the same condition.

Studying and checking his Herb Bible on a daily basis, which was beginning to look thumb-worn and tattered, I now found my kitchen and bathroom cupboards burdened with spices, herbs and lotions of all kinds. I did not complain about this, but drew the line when asked to bake scones and cookies using stevia, which originated from Paraguay, as a sweetener, many times sweeter than sugar, plus some dreadful grey-looking flour, the name of which I had never heard. Using these ingredients made scones turn out like concrete-hard rock buns. I envisaged not only Rowland's teeth but mine breaking on these scones. The idea of losing any teeth, to eat these "healing" scones, was not on my agenda.

The cookies were the ones I hated baking most of all as they had the worst taste unimaginable and were the final assault on the reputation of one who baked and cooked to near perfection, seeing time and effort thrown into the garbage bin. Forever conscious if you don't succeed the first time, try, and try again, I plodded on! But further efforts proved futile, so finally I gave up.

After much soul-searching I realized cookies baked with these ingredients were doomed from the start, as no palate could possibly be enticed to eat them. Thereafter, I suggested buying cookies from the Health Food store. Rowland made no comment when these purchases were made, and tucked into them with relish.

A favourite dish was curried chicken or shrimp and on one occasion when I cooked this for dinner, Rowland commented that the flavour wasn't strong enough and asked if I would add turmeric to an extra spoonful of Madras curry on future menus, which I did.

At one sitting, as we began eating dinner of chicken curry and rice, I almost choked laughing at the pained expression on his face while noticing at the same time, his forehead was showing beads of perspiration. I could see the effect the curry was having on him, as his face now took on the colour of beet-red.

'Too hot for you?' I asked, suppressing the urge to laugh.

'Try it,' was his response, holding his hand to his throat.

Doing as he bid I put my fork into the curry dish, swallowed, and felt I was on fire. I couldn't speak and gasping for breath, tears flooded my eyes. I rushed into the kitchen to get cold drinks. Needless to say, this episode of adding turmeric with additional curry powder was never repeated. And, furthermore, they were sparingly used on future menus, despite Rowland saying he liked it, 'Hot, hot!'

We were now at a point when regular teas were replaced by Organic Rooibos tea, the plant of which is found in the Cedarberg Mountains of South Africa's Cape Province and harvested during the hot African summer for peak flavour. While Rowland enjoyed drinking it, I found the taste very bitter.

Another fad was bread made without yeast, which took precedent over wheat bread. This type was more expensive than the normal bread one usually buys and, again, not in tune with my palate. Sampling these experiments of herbs, teas and bread, was an exercise in the art of patience and understanding; meanwhile, I wondered where it would all end.

Yogurt, another item in his diet, he couldn't get enough of. When grocery shopping we bought several different flavoured yogurts, which were placed on the top shelf in the refrigerator. Many times I would see Rowland roaming round the house, dessert spoon in hand, devouring mouthfuls of yogurt out of the container. When I first saw him doing this I suggested getting a dessert bowl but he shunned that idea saying, 'It's better this way.' I couldn't argue, seeing the happy look on his face.

Often, when visiting his doctor, Rowland would immediately tell the doctor what herb he used to heal a particular pain. Paranoia convinced him that suffering with candida was the cause of all his problems, but tests proved otherwise. While the doctor listened, the chatter went on about how he was curing certain ailments, with specific herbs. Knowing this was the very reason why he was seeing the doctor in the first place, with the same complaint, the urge to nudge Rowland and tell him to let the doctor make his diagnosis, had no effect. I would look at the doctor, and he in turn knew what I was trying to convey to him, without uttering a word. By the time we reached home I didn't know whether to laugh or cry, as I realized Rowland was quite incorrigible. There would be no "curing" him of these habits and beliefs.

YEAR ROUND SANTA

With his never-ending generosity Rowland was never happier when giving gifts of money or presents, particularly to small children. He exuded euphoria and had the adrenaline flowing when any onlooker watched him put his hand out tenderly to a young child. Not only was the mother affected by this warm gesture, but anyone else standing by.

If a child on the other side of the street was crying, Rowland would make a bee-line, cross over, and gently ask, 'What's the matter? Can we make it better?'

With the mother looking on to determine what this complete stranger was all about, perhaps interfering, Rowland explained he didn't like hearing a child cry. Thinking it might stop the tears, Rowland would put a coin or two into the child's hand, with endearing words, 'You like sweeties, don't you?'

Of course a Canadian child hadn't a clue what he meant by "sweeties" and would look at Rowland with wide-tearful eyes, while clutching the coins in his hands. I explained to Rowland that sweets in Canada were known as "candies" and if he wanted to give children money to buy some, it would be a good idea to say candies.

I also tactfully suggested that before giving any child money, perhaps he should ask the parent's permission first, so that his gift was not misinterpreted as being given for some unsavoury reason. Rowland understood what I was trying to convey to him, and totally agreed with me.

Many times, especially at Christmas and Easter, if we were in a store where toys were sold and he heard a young boy ask his mother for a particular item, which she couldn't afford it, seeing the disappointed look on the child's face he would go up to the mother and ask if he could pay for it. With a reticent look on her face, perhaps doubting the offer made, and seeing the eager look on her child's upturned face, she would eventually agree. When the purchase of the toy was made and it was safely in the child's hands, not only did the mother thank him for his kindness, but so also did a smiling, happy boy.

We would often see one particular mother, whom we met at the Mothers & Babies group with two of her children at her side. One of the little girls who christened us "Mama and Papa" was a delight to behold! Whenever we spotted them in the drug store Rowland made sure they had candies, and if there was a particular toy or book that interested them, he would buy it. Seeing happy faces, jumping with joy, was enough for him, as we waved goodbye when leaving the store.

A young, single mother, with two small children, was often given a hundred dollars to buy food. We both knew this good, caring mother was struggling to make ends meet, so Rowland not only bought food for the family but also clothes and toys for the children. He never forgot them at Christmas time.

These occasions with mothers and children were to continue for the rest of my brother's life. He excelled at making children happy and to see a child cry, affected him deeply.

Our trips into Victoria was another venue where Rowland would do the "Santa" thing. Always on the side of the underdog, when stopping off outside the Eaton's Centre, if he heard the jingle, jingle of the Salvation Army bells the first thing he would do was to pull out a ten or twenty dollar note from his wallet and put it into their donation box.

The Salvation Army in Victoria was not the only recipient of his generosity. If he spotted donation boxes for charity anywhere, and heard jingling bells, he would willingly donate as much as possible, 'for a worthy cause', as he put it, adding, 'We are well aware of the wonderful work the Salvation Army and other charitable organizations do, not only here, but in other parts of the world.'

My brother never forgot the day when he received a letter in 1990 from the Salvation Army's office in London, England, saying a sister was looking for him who lived on the other side of the world. It was their efforts that enabled us to finally get in touch with one another. His praise of them for their tremendous work was unfaltering. Years ago, I promised him that I would continue to make a yearly donation to the Salvation Army on behalf of us both. It is his way of thanking them.

Another situation that affected him immensely was seeing young "street people" when we got off the bus at the Eaton's Centre in Victoria. He would stop and chat to different groups who were sitting on rugs or blankets, with dogs sleeping close to them. On one occasion a young girl, who looked to be in her twenties, approached him, pleading poverty. Without doubting her needs, he handed her a twenty dollar note and told her to get something to eat. After the girl thanked him we began walking toward the Centre, when a lady tapped him on the shoulder.

'You shouldn't be giving money to that girl,' said the stranger. 'I know her family who live in Oak Bay and are comfortably well-off. She has no right to ask you for money.'

Rowland was dumfounded, and responded, 'If I wish to give money to anyone, that is my privilege.'

The woman strode off, in a huff!

That Rowland was a year-round Santa made him feel good. At Christmas, he never forgot our postman, or the men who picked up household and garden waste at the house.

He didn't expect anything in return, but gave freely gifts of money or toys to the children and also to the needy.

CLOSER TO TOWN

In 2004, we decided to move into a condominium as we could no longer keep up the maintenance on the house and garden where we'd lived together for seven years.

Rowland was finding the garden work too much and I did not want him stressed out, knowing how particular he was with his manicured lawns and keeping weed-free flower beds, a joy for all to see. It wasn't a move we took lightly as we knew we would miss the neighbourhood, also the people we had come to know who frequently passed the house. Our postman, in particular, we deemed a friend who would stop and chat for a few minutes when delivering the mail.

Another reason for changing residences was because my car died a natural death and to buy a new one did not appeal to me. Without the car it meant either taking a taxi or walking into town for grocery shopping. Either way, we found it time-consuming and tiring. Living in town we were able to walk to the shops, and also deal with other necessities more easily such as the bank, post office, dentist or doctor. Nearby bus stops for day trips into and out of Victoria was another factor that appealed to us.

Our local transit finally awakened to the call that residents needed more buses into the city, hospital and airport. Population in Sidney was

9,000 when I arrived here in 1987, and by 2004 had increased to nearly 13,000, which meant additional vehicles on the roads causing traffic to become highly congested. Development was another consideration, and as more houses and condominiums were being built then at reasonable prices, people were drifting in from other provinces to live in an area with a more temperate climate. Noticeably, many retired couples from Alberta settled here. Travelling on buses avoided the problem of trying to find parking space when going into Victoria.

During this period Rowland was now finding the need of an orthopaedic doctor to have fluid on his knees frequently drained, either at the doctor's office or the local hospital. Sometimes this treatment worked for a while; he was also having shots of cortisone in the knees. However the condition returned, making it painful for him to walk. I often wondered if this could be the result of when his ship caught fire during World War Two and from the blast, being thrown from the wheelhouse up against the rear wall of the chart room. This incident caused him to suffer with extreme back pain in later years.

My brother who always identified himself as a "swallow," loving the heat and sunshine. He was not shy at seventy-five years of age to don short, shorts and "fly" around town, legs, knees and thighs, bare for all to see. Often I would say to him, 'Those shorts, Row, are really too much. You are revealing flesh that might embarrass the local ladies.'

'Oh, no, dear,' was his response, 'I'm sure they would tell me if I insulted them by showing too much leg.'

I left that unanswered, as I couldn't find the words.

I realized the charmer he was, so why not wear what you wish in your golden years. In any case, I did not have the right to dictate what type of clothes he wore.

However, at times smartly dressed with collar, tie and jacket, even in the hot weather, it was a standing joke with a local friend of ours who owns a coffee shop, that Rowland could always be relied upon to look well-groomed when we dropped by his place for coffee.

Whenever we went into Victoria to attend the Question Period held at the legislature we first ate lunch, then ambled past the Empress Hotel toward the government buildings and entered the public gallery. These sessions could be a lengthy ordeal for the general public to have to sit and list to rhetorical speakers with, what we thought, little achieved. After attending several sessions we were of the opinion our afternoons were better spent elsewhere.

Although interested to a degree in certain political issues, Rowland was not quite enthused as I was. I mentioned to him how different politics were in British Columbia, compared to Ontario. Here, I sensed lethargy with our ministers, who appeared to have neither energy or time when contacted for a direct answer to a direct problem, which left me wondering if the letters I sent them were worth the effort on my part.

Of the two Premiers of Ontario, Bill Davis and Dalton McGinty, to whom I wrote on several occasions, the letters I received from them was not of the formula-type but written with information on how government would address these issues. This left the citizen with the assured feeling that both premiers would give their attention to these matters.

TRIP TO ENGLAND

In 2006 Rowland and I booked a flight to England, where we hoped to stay with our own families for a month. On the day we were due to leave Victoria International airport, after waiting an appreciable time in the departure lounge, we were advised by an airline staff member that no flights would be leaving that evening, due to a computer breakdown.

We were asked to go home and return at a certain time the next day. Explaining to the Air Canada staff member that we had a connecting flight from Vancouver to Heathrow, London, and would miss it, she said, 'Don't worry, you will be taken care of.' Added to this set-back was the fact we had family meeting us at Heathrow, which no doubt would concern them if the plane did not arrive on time. Assuring us this can all be dealt with once the computer problem has been resolved, we left the airport and returned home.

Seeing the disappointed look on Rowland's face when we arrived home, I suggested a light meal and early night so we could be well-rested for tomorrow's flight. At the same time, we were trusting we would finally get off the ground and arrive safely at Heathrow.

Next morning our taxi took us back to the airport, where large crowds were lined up, all looking anxious as to whether they would or would not be able to board the Vancouver flight. We had absolutely no idea of knowing if seats had been allocated to us on both flights, but my concerns were allayed when an Air Canada staff member drew us to one side and gave us boarding passes. She explained that when we arrive at Vancouver we present the passes to another staff member who would see us on the London flight. Upon landing, we were ushered aboard the aircraft bound for Heathrow and pleasantly surprised to find we had been put in first class seats!

Throughout the journey we were offered food and drinks, and provided with excellent service. Settling down in a comfortable seat, I relaxed, and hoped to get a few hours sleep before landing. Rowland, on the other hand, was restless. He ate little, and proceeded to pace the aisle up and down the aircraft which had me worried. He may have slept a little, I don't know, as I was well into slumberland after enjoying a pleasant dinner.

When I awoke Rowland was standing up, rather than sitting. I asked him if he was all right as he appeared agitated, like a cat on hot bricks, but he assured me he was fine.

'Come and sit down,' I urged.

His unusual behaviour of standing and not sitting, when flying, was out of character for him. Normally, when in an aircraft, he would down a Bailey's Irish Cream and nod peacefully off to sleep until landing. This time it was different.

Needless to say, when we got off the plane at Heathrow, Rowland was exhausted. With the help of a porter we gathered our luggage and waited near the information centre for our family to pick us up.

Looking around I muttered, 'I think we're in the wrong airport.' All I could see were men with turbans on their heads and women in long garments, wearing yashmaks over their faces.

'We're at the right place,' responded Rowland. 'This is what England now looks like.'

After we waited close to half an hour for Rowland's family to arrive, they explained the delay was due to the problem of finding a parking place for the car. After lots of hugging, we drove from Heathrow to Hampshire where I would spend the month with William, our younger brother.

Almost a week had passed before we received a phone call from Rowland. Because of the weakness in his voice, I asked him if he was feeling all right.

'No, not really,' he replied.

In response, I suggested it might be good idea for him to get plenty of rest but knew that when visiting family in England they were forever on the trot going here, there and everywhere, so for him to rest at all would prove difficult.

Apparently when arriving at his daughter's home he was told that because his son-in-law's father had recently passed away, he and his wife would have to leave immediately to attend the funeral in Yorkshire, in the North of England.

Rowland found himself in a strange house, in strange surroundings. To catch up on some much-needed sleep he went to bed and some hours later, awakened in a state of disorientation. Picking up the telephone for help, he was asked his name, and from where he was speaking.

'I don't know,' he said.

Asking the same questions the operator repeated, 'Give us your name.'

Again he replied, 'I don't know.'

A short time later an ambulance arrived but there is some confusion how they entered the front door of the house, to take him to Basingstoke General Hospital, where he remained for a week.

William and I had no idea what had happened with Rowland and his family, and were rather shocked with this piece of news. At the same time, I looked back at his behaviour on the flight over, and wondered if this had any bearing on his present health condition.

We chatted for a bit, and said we hoped he would be able to enjoy the rest of his stay with his family.

'I will see you at Heathrow, when we return to Canada,' I quipped, little realizing we were to meet sooner, in Hampshire.

WILLIAM: A BORN GAMBLER 1924–2007

Eighteen months older than me, William decided to join the Royal Navy when he reached the age of seventeen, as he was not only anxious to do his bit for the war effort but also to get away from a boring life of working on a farm, which was considered essential work. William had been raised in an orphanage, and it was typical for boys to be assigned in church-owned farms as soon as they were sixteen. Joining the Navy was one of the few routes out of that rough labour.

Slightly built, with a head of jet-black hair, his exuberant nature ensured life for him would be anything but dull. Never having put a cigarette to his lips prior to joining the Navy, to keep his mates company, he took to drinking and smoking with great gusto and went eagerly "for the ride" into town on the look-out for the nearest dance hall or pub, girls included.

While discipline was rigidly enforced, he found life in the Navy suited him admirably. Whenever he came home on leave, with his cap perched at the back of his head, and in his bell-bottom trousers, he would swing in and out of local pubs as though he owned them. Completely blasé with the world around him and determined to enjoy every hour of his leave, relatives wondered if this sailor would ever be normal again.

When William first joined the Royal Navy in 1941, he remembered

William, Naval Rating, 1945.

how he was forced to swim. An officer separated the ship's crew into swimmers and non-swimmers, and when the number of non-swimmers was in place, each man was tossed into the ocean and told to swim. William said he thought he would drown, as he had no idea what to do with his arms and legs. The officer on watch, standing over the side of the ship, was shouting instructions to the men in the water, determined to make every man a swimmer. Conscious of bad language being bandied about, and knowing he wasn't coming aboard at least until the preliminaries were understood, William tried the dog-paddle, which didn't work, so struck out with arms and leg flailing in all direction, with the result he found himself swimming. Grinning widely when telling me his story of how he came to be a swimmer, he chuckled, 'Only the Navy could toss men in the ocean and get away with it.'

I asked him if this was on a one-time basis when he and his companions were thrown into the ocean.

'No, we were thrown in a few times and the exercises only stopped when the officer satisfied himself that non-swimmers were now swimmers. We had to learn fast, knowing lives are in danger if the ship goes down.'

When on shore leave he headed to the Playhouse in Walton-on-Thames, where weekly dances took place Friday and Saturday nights. It was here he met a dark-haired beauty named Violet, whom he began courting. At every opportunity they would meet, go dancing, or hire a boat and row on the River Thames, stopping halfway for a cool drink at one of the riverside pubs. The Swan, a favourite pub habitually crowded with servicemen, provided the publican with a healthy living. His wife, Irene, was a forty-year-old brassy-blonde, whose full luscious lips were covered with brilliant red lipstick and her face plastered with heavy make-up; where this came from during rationing, is anyone's guess. Certainly it didn't look like the lipstick most factory girls used that came from old stubs left over in their lipstick holders, which they pooled together and melted down in a metal pot, to provide them with a lipstick of sorts.

With their on-going philosophy of "live for the day," servicemen from Allied countries and local residents alike could be heard singing, dancing and swilling many pints of beer well into the night. Spending two shillings and sixpence for a tot of gin for the ladies was never far behind the pints that spilled over the bar counter.

'Time, please,' from the publican, with bell in hand, went ignored. No one took the slightest notice. Even the local police appeared to turn a blind eye, perhaps thinking this might be some of these men's last night. Then, gradually, before leaving the pub, the servicemen with girls hanging on their arms could be heard singing, 'Goodnight, Irene, goodnight.'

To this day, I can only guess with the selection of food the publican

William and Violet.

was able to provide, which he sold at black-market prices to his customers, that it came from locally-based army camps. To even think of questioning his conduct blacklisted you from the pub.

Occasionally, when on leave, William, Violet and I would go to The Swan for a drink. One could always be sure of the pub being packed, with knees and elbows touching. Normally, a non-drinker, I sat with them over a glass of orange juice, then William would set us off laughing at some malarkey that went on down in his ship's engine room, where he worked, while cautiously aware that secret talk could put one in jail. When the second set of drinks came round, and this happened the first time, I was somewhat surprised to see that mine was a port and lemon and said to William, 'You know I don't drink.'

To which he replied, 'Try something different for a change, I'm sure you will like it.'

Cautiously sipping the drink I found it tasted quite pleasant; in fact, I was beginning to feel comfortably warm, then I began to giggle.

'Does it always have this effect on you?' I asked.

'Sometimes,' came the response, with a cigarette drooping from his lips, 'depends on how much of it you drink.'

From that day on I was hooked on port and lemon and when asked what I'd like to drink my request was, 'Usual, please.'

'There,' said William, rather cockily, 'knew you'd like it.'

After a few months of courting and with the realization William could be shipped overseas at any given time, he and Violet decided to get married. When I first met Violet I took to her immediately. She was a shy, gentle person, of medium height with shoulder-length black curly hair. Although I sensed a remarkable difference in their make-up I could see Violet blending her personality with the exuberant nature of her husband's, whom I'm sure would have her lovingly dancing to his tune.

At the end of the war William left the Royal Navy and returned to civvy street, where jobs were few and far between. Adjusting to civilian life did not exactly appeal to him; he missed the camaraderie of his fellow shipmates and although he tried to be supportive to his wife, he was like a fish out of water. Realizing the transition difficulty from service to civilian life William now faced, Violet told him she would not stand in his way if he wished to rejoin the Navy.

In 1947, back in uniform and once again on the high seas, William travelled to many British overseas naval ports. His shore bases were Plymouth, Portsmouth, Chatham and Lowestoft. Periodically his ship docked at Greenock, 21 miles westnorthwest of Glasgow, Scotland with extensive docks and according to William, a "freezing hole." Whenever on home base in Portsmouth and due for leave, he didn't have far to travel to see his wife who lived in a small town nearby. Portsmouth is the chief British naval base, in southeast Hampshire, on Portsea Island, 65 miles southwest of London, at entrance to Portsmouth Harbour on the Spithead. *H.M.S. Victory*, Nelson's flagship at Trafalgar, is preserved here in dry dock. In 1940-41 during the Second World War, the city suffered heavy air raids.

While William was serving in Malta in 1948, he received news Violet had given birth to a son, whom they christened David. Sixteen months later, another son was born, named Paul.

A period of nine years elapsed when Violet discovered to her surprise she was once again pregnant and gave birth to a daughter who was christened after William's sister, Kathleen. At the time of this happy event he was overseas, and ecstatic when hearing the news he had a daughter. Knowing the exuberance of his nature, I'm sure he wet the baby's head in great style not once, but twice.

Having risen to the rank of Petty Officer Engineer, he trained young Naval cadets in the mechanics of engineering who addressed him as, 'Sir.' However, when they passed all exams and became officers, the boot was on the other foot. William in true Navy tradition, reversed the saluting by addressing them, 'Sir.' It always amused him by this turn of events, particularly if he noticed an officer hesitate in the engine room as though unsure which way to tackle a problem. Having taught him in the first place how engines functioned, although he had not been ordered to do so, he would advise the officer of the correct procedure how to keep the engines running. This did not go down well with one officer, who wanted to do things his way. William saw the funny side to this and said to himself, 'He'll soon learn, mistakes or otherwise. When he comes a cropper, no doubt he'll come searching for me; until then, he's on his own.'

Hearing him talk of his Navy days I often wondered how he managed to hold onto his Petty Officer rank as once or twice, when the ship docked at certain ports for a few days, William decided he had earned the right to go off and have a good time with whomever he met on dry land. In so doing, and thoroughly enjoying himself with all and sundry, completely forgetting the time, on two occasions he missed his ship.

Problem, problem, how was he going to explain to his captain how this came about, and by what means would he be able to find the location of his ship? He never divulged the outcome of these events to me, so I was left to guess what transpired between him and his captain. Keeping strictly to Naval rule, I don't think William could talk his way out of this one.

The history of *H.MS. Amethyst* goes back to 1949, when she was on her way from Shanghai to Nanjing on the Yangtze River to replace *H.M.S. Consort*, which was standing as guard ship there for the British Embassy due to the war between the People's Liberation Army and the Chinese Communists. As the frigate came further up the river, she came under heavy fire from the P.L.A. battery. By the time the shelling stopped *Amethyst* had received over 50 hits and holes below the waterline were plugged with bedding and hammocks.

Amethyst was under guard by the P.L.A. for ten weeks, with vital supplies being withheld from the ship. On July 30, 1949 *Amethyst* slipped her chains and headed downriver in the dark, while running the gauntlet of Communist guns on both banks of the river. She made contact with *H.M.S. Consort* on August 11, 1949.

William mentioned that during his service in 1949 his ship was on the Yangtze River at the time of this conflict between the P.L.A. and the Communists, but did not mentioned the name of the ship on which he served.

I have a photo of *H.M.S. Euryalus* which my brother was on entering Malta Harbour in 1948. He did not elaborate if *Euryalus* was one of the ships on the Yangtze River in 1949. He did tell me, however, the situation on the Yangtze was extremely critical and it was touch and go if the ship and crew would get out alive. Reading between the lines and listening to him describe how things happened during this period, my guess is that he was on the Yangtze but perhaps on another ship, otherwise how could his vision of the conflict be so descriptive.

In recognition of service, the Royal Navy awarded medals to all naval personnel who served in ships on the Yangtze River. As my late

Above: 1960.

Below: H.M.S. Euryalus, *March 30, 1948.*

brother's Navy medals are now in the possession of his eldest son, I am unable to substantiate if William was a recipient of this medal.

In 1969, after twenty-two years in the Royal Navy, William finally left the service and eventually settled down in civvy life to support his family. By this time I had emigrated to Canada and saw little of his children growing up, unless I was back in England on a visit. Elizabeth and I would then take the train from London to see them. The children adored their Aunt Elizabeth, a gentle loving soul, whose kindness to them knew no bounds whenever she visited them, despite having little money for herself.

As the children were growing up and at school during the day, Violet decided to take work as a 'Lolly Pop' lady. Wearing a yellow jacket and carrying in her hand a stop sign, she would see the children coming out of school safely across the road. She enjoyed doing this job for a number of reasons and over the years earned herself extra pounds which enabled her not only to purchase a small scooter, but also to socialize with other mothers living in the district. Eventually, she gave up being a 'Lolly Pop' lady but kept her scooter, as this was her only means of getting from place to place and doing her shopping.

Over the years, William noticed his wife was gradually becoming thinner and thinner. Although she never carried much weight, even after the children were born, this loss of weight had him extremely worried, so he made an appointment for her to see the doctor. After tests were done, the doctor told him they showed the oesophagus narrowing and that with this condition it prevented solid food passing from the mouth to the stomach, causing difficulty in swallowing and weight loss. With his advice a procedure was recommended to correct the problem but this lasted a short time, after which it was necessary to repeat the procedure. When this didn't work a decision was made to insert a plastic tube into the throat, in the hope she would be able to swallow solid food. However again, it was unsuccessful. At this time, the doctor surprised William with the news that Violet's condition, in being unable to properly absorb food, went back to her childhood.

Sadly, Violet's weight loss continued and the only food she could manage to eat was either mashed or in liquid form. The last time I saw her it saddened me to see her looking so ill and while William did all he could for her, her health declined rapidly.

She was a caring mother who put her children first before her own needs and had a tremendous sense of humour. I don't know anyone who could use so many puns, direct and indirect, leaving one laughing, uncontrollably. Violet passed away in December 1990 and was cremated in Winchester, Hampshire, 60 miles southwest of London, England.

I remember on a number of occasions travelling by coach from William's home in Waterlooville to Winchester. It is a two-hour journey both ways, so leaves little time to look and search for historical landmarks. The great cathedral founded in 1079 by Bishop Walkelin contains tombs of bishops Edington, Wykeham, Waynflete, of some Danish and Saxon kings, and Jane Austen.

Before heading into Winchester historical attractions, I shopped, then stopped at a restaurant to eat. I was browsing through the town and about to enter a large department store, when a gypsy selling sprigs of heather, among other things, gave me a gentle shove. As I turned to look at her, she spieled out her tale of woe. I was about to dip into my wallet when out of the blue, she disappeared. Looking up I noticed a policeman walking towards me, but he passed without saying a word. I wondered what caused the gypsy to disappear so quickly. Were there repercussions for selling goods without a licence? Certainly the heather wasn't bringing her the promised good luck.

When I returned home, I told William what happened with the gypsy.

'Oh,' he remarked, 'because the shop-keepers keep complaining, the police are trying to stop the gypsies from coming into Winchester pestering the visitors and local residents alike.'

I remarked to him that on each visit I made to England, I noticed the odd one or two gypsy popping up in cities, rather than their normal habitat, the country. I then went on to tell him of the incident in Arundel.

'Not surprised,' was his comment, 'but they're not really harming anyone, are they?'

We chatted about the days when we were growing up in Kent and watched, in awe, many gypsies strolling down the long country lanes. Children were nowhere to be seen, while the men and womenfolk walked in front of their caravans, with metal tins dangling and clanging on the backs of them. Once they selected a field to rest, the caravans painted in brilliant reds and greens were set down and within minutes, the men had huge fires burning in front of them. With long, white pipes the men sat smoking, while the women were busy cooking in large black pots. I would think it highly unlikely that when choosing a field, the gypsies asked the owners for permission to come on their land, perhaps with thoughts that the fields of nature belonged to everyone.

During my school days I saw a great number of these gypsies, especially on outings, where we walked for miles to study Earth's nature. When we passed the fields and had the urge to stop and peek through a hole in the hawthorne hedges that edged the lanes, we were too afraid to even tie a shoelace or dawdle behind, as we heard tales that gypsies, whom we knew as Tinkers, stole children who were never seen again. Was this true or false? We dared not put it to the test.

The Romany gypsies, as they are known, are believed to be of Indian origin and their Romany language related to Hindustani. In 1417, they appeared in Western Europe, gradually finding their way to England in the 16th century. With dark skins, large black eyes, black hair, they are born wanderers who roam from place to place and are known as tinkers, basket-makers, among other things. These gypsies are not only a resilient race but extremely cunning, and when the need to feed themselves and their families arises they will go to any length to survive.

It was common in the Kent area that a farmer would expect to find himself missing a complete patch of cabbages or potatoes, which the gypsies had stolen and sold without remorse to unsuspected buyers. When hearing of these incidences that went on for years, with farmers suffering heavy losses, I must confess I held a certain respect for the gypsies' tenacity. To go unnoticed in the night, probably in groups, to steal and sell, takes courage. The consequences of being caught red-handed with the farmer's crops would, no doubt, require a full explanation to the law.

When visiting England, in later years, apart from seeing the odd one or two, most of the gypsies have disappeared. These were colourful people, with beautifully decorated caravans, did no real harm, even though most young children lived in fear of being caught and kept by them.

A few months had gone by since Violet passed away, and when speaking with William over the telephone, I asked him how he was faring. We chatted for a bit, then he told me Violet not only had a tremendous sense of humour but also a stubborn streak to her nature. I was rather surprised with the news as, somehow, I could not see her like this. But he told me that at one time he was offered a position in the Australian Navy to teach engineering to young cadets, where he and his family would be provided with accommodation, and he could earn a substantial income. Putting the proposal to Violet, there and then she refused to take herself and her children to, as she put it, 'a backward country,' also adding, 'I don't want to leave friends and neighbours.'

On another occasion when William wanted to emigrate to Canada her determined streak surfaced once again so he backed down with the idea and from then on, all other notions of going abroad were put on the back burner.

William was a good family man who loved his children dearly and when his grandchildren came along, he spoiled them rotten. Often, when one sat on his lap, I watched from the corner of my eye the way he tucked his hand into his pocket for candy, which he quickly popped into the child's mouth before Mother could see. I'm sure this memory of Granddad's generosity will remain with them throughout their years. If one was near the kitchen while William was cooking dinner, with a forked prong he speared a roasted potato on the end, and handed it to the child.

'Hot,' he would say, 'don't burn your mouth.'

The bright look on the child's face was magic to the eye.

On a yearly basis I visited William, now living alone in Hampshire, for a month. Not far from where he lived was the golf club, where we often dined. One evening, walking in semi-darkness within a short distance from his house, we ambled along arm-in-arm toward the club when suddenly we were stopped in our tracks by a red tail fox walking across our path that took not the slightest notice of us. It would be one of many occasions when we saw the fox out for its evening stroll. The first time this happened, I whispered to William, 'What was that!'

'One of our local residents,' came the reply.

When taking daily walks I often went into the nearby parkland, where parts of it were closed off with a high chain-link fence. Whether this was supposed to keep out the foxes is questionable because on every walkabout, within two feet of the fence, I saw many red tail foxes resting or generally standing, staring outward. Often, I stopped to watch them with their pointed noses and sharp eyes looking in my direction, while at the same time admiring their bushy long tails and hoping they would not charge the fence.

Oddly enough, when walking halfway round the perimeter of the parkland I noticed the fence stopped there, with openings at both ends, which allowed the foxes entry to come and go as they pleased. It struck me as being odd why the fence was put there in the first place, when it was open to birds and animals to stray at will. The foxes appeared quite familiar with people as they wandered in and out of residential areas, with a calm and casual presence, while the locals looked on as though this was part of their normal lives.

Seemingly passive in nature, one can only envisage how scared these animals must be when the hunters and hounds are chasing them during

At left, William in his Petty Officer uniform, serving abroad in the 1960s. The photo below was taken in Singapore in 1961.

a fox hound event. The inevitable result leaves little to the imagination, with empathy on the side of the fox.

On a first night visiting William, I heard the most horrendous screaming in the early hours of the morning and couldn't sleep for the noise. When I mentioned this the next day to William he said, 'Oh, it's nothing to worry about. It often happens when a fox is protecting its mate and territory, the screaming begins and could go on all night.'

'Is this a seasonal occurrence, or does it happen on the odd occasion?' I questioned William.

'Don't know,' was the dry response, 'they come and go when it suits them.' He added, 'They are all over Hampshire, tame as can be, and breed like wildfire.'

A man of great fun, who didn't take the world seriously, he loved to gamble as he put it, 'on the gee-gees' and like Rowland, loved a good joke. Coming from William some jokes were rather risqué.

'Navy jokes?' I quipped.

'Yep,' came the laughing response.

Forever the gambler William would take me into town on race day to place bets at the bookies on his choice of runners. Epsom Downs horse races, known as The Derby, was founded 1780 and named for the Earl of Derby. This yearly event not only sees royalty wearing colourful hats but ladies of wealth in general donning large fancy headgear all competing with one another and the more outrageous, the better. At Doncaster, West Riding, South Yorkshire on Don River, the St. Leger stakes, a race course founded in 1776, is for three-year-olds.

Never one to overspend his money where gambling was concerned, he would put twenty pence on each line, to win, choosing many of the horses not considered favourites; all of them had peculiar names, but he bet on them anyway and ultimately claimed a prize between five to ten pounds sterling. If he won on several horses for twenty pence a line, he could pick up between thirty to one hundred pounds sterling, much to the bookie's consternation. The bookies never made much money out of William, who chuckled loudly: 'Next bet is paid for by them.'

I don't think I've ever known any gambler to put so little money on horses and win most of the time.

On my visit in 2006, William told me he was beginning to lose the sight in one of his eyes, and asked me to help him fill out a bookie's slip. Under his tuition I was beginning to get the hang on how to make them out and when he didn't feel like going into town himself he would send me by taxi to place the bets for him. When he decided what horses to bet on and how much on each of them he was willing to gamble, before I had time to begin calculating the amount needed, in a flash his mathematical brain would give me the exact figure. He never ceased to amaze me how quickly he could work out a mathematical problem and however hard I tried to catch him out, I never could. Sometimes when trying to get the right numbers on a bookie's slip, I would grumble to William when he threw the answer up at me, saying to him, 'You don't give me a chance, even to think.'

'Sorry, thought you needed help with the money, as our currency is different to yours,' was his response.

'In Canada, we deal in cents, too,' I remarked, 'didn't you know?'

Looking at me, he mumbled, 'Okay, we'll use your brain power, next race.'

When first entering the bookie shop I was nervous at seeing so many men intent on playing the horses and dogs, and was almost blinded by a thick haze of cigarette smoke the minute you entered their domain. But, eventually, I became friendly with a few of them who gave me good tips on the horses running. Putting the odd bob or two on a horse tip given to me by one of the gamblers, I usually ended up with a win and when mentioning it to William he said, 'Beginner's luck.'

It would be one of my many wins, which had him chuckling!

Like Rowland, William was an exceptional cook. Every time I stayed with him in Hampshire I knew, without fail, Sunday roast dinners would be so gargantuan, that inwardly, I groaned at the size of portions put on my plate. Vegetables of all kinds, plus roast potatoes, were piled high with meat of the day. If that wasn't enough to whet the appetite, Yorkshire puddings were added, over which cascaded hot, thick gravy. No one could make Yorkshire puddings like William. They rose like puffy clouds, and although I used his recipe many times, I did not get the same results. Not to offend him I ate whatever dinners he placed before me, with certain relish, but halfway through the meal, imagined I would "blow up." Not surprisingly, when returning home to Canada, I bulged with considerable weight and had to squeeze into my clothes. Rowland, on the other hand, in his seventies, could down large meals without putting on an ounce of fat. Where he put it all, left me wondering.

Whenever I planned a visit, spring or fall, with William he booked a week's holiday at the Crown Hotel in Weymouth, and we had the time of our life. He always chose a room overlooking the ocean, which he knew pleased me. The hotel is situated near the harbour and the beach, theatre, bowling, fishing trips, sea cruises and the bird sanctuary are all within walking distance. In addition to its charm and character, the standard of food served in the hotel restaurant is highly recommended.

What I noticed during my yearly visits to the Crown was that the staff remained unchanged and be it in the restaurant, bars or taking care of one's room, everyone was friendly and helpful to visitors. The manager, a delightful person, had an ear for everyone. Running his hotel like a tight ship enabled him to maintain a regular staff, with little turnover. He would often chat with William in the bar on a variety of subjects and although they were two entirely different characters, they appeared to hit it off well.

The attractive seaside resort of Weymouth lies on the south English coast, just south of Dorchester, known as the Dorset Riviera. It has beaches of whiter sand, clearer, warmer water, although even on the warmest of days the water can be bracing. Knowing few tourists would be on the beach in the early hours of the morning I walked along the shoreline, breathing in the salty air, while conscious of every step I took the warm, gritty sand would impact between my toes.

One early instance of Weymouth's notoriety is that in 1348 it served as the point of entry in Britain for the black death, the plague that killed a third of Europe's population. The oldest tavern in Weymouth is reputed to be The Black Dog.

Weymouth's port served as the launching spot for more than 500,000 troops and nearly 150,000 vehicles during the D-Day landings in 1944. Nearby Portland was the base of battleships *Nelson, Rodney, Ramillies* and *Warspite*.

William, like Rowland, was a generous man and couldn't give enough. Often we would take the bus from Weymouth into Dorchester, a few miles away, a city bustling with history. We would lunch at one of the old pubs, and then shop around town.

If there was anything I fancied he would immediately put his hand in his pocket and buy it for me. I usually headed for the Edinburgh Wool shop because of quality and fashion, and if there was a particular item I liked, William would encourage me to take two.

'Just in case, you need them,' was his comment.

I couldn't argue with him that I really only needed one to wear at a time, and not two. He was not to be put off.

We would take in a show at the Weymouth local theatre then meander, with all the time in the world, back to the hotel for a drink. If he saw anyone he knew in the bar, William treated them also to a nightcap.

The ferries from Weymouth have daily trips to Guernsey, the second largest of Channel Islands, 28 miles west of the Normandy coast at Saint Peter Port, where they dock and allow passengers to get off and spend an hour or two, to shop. The island is famous for its fine cattle.

Victor Hugo, dramatist, poet and novelist who headed the Romantic movement in France in the early part of the 19th century, in his later years while living in exile in Guernsey wrote his famous novel *Les Misérables*. He lived at St. Peter Port for over 15 years.

Jersey, the largest and southernmost of Channel Islands, is 15 miles west of Normandy coast and 18 miles southeast of Guernsey. Here the ferry docks at St. Helier.

The inhabitants on these islands are mostly of Norman descent. English, French and local dialects are spoken.

During the Second World War, the Islands were invaded by the Germans who created fear and hardship to the local inhabitants, most of whom were farmers. Orders were given to them that all food grown in the fields was to be handed over to the enemy, to feed their armies. Many farmers, however, risked their lives by digging large underground burrows and buried whatever vegetables they could, so their families would not starve. The consequence of disobeying an order resulted in the farmer being shot if caught. Like most countries who endured the enemy's tyrannical control, it was a terrifying time for the peoples of Jersey and Guernsey, whose only need in life was undisturbed peace.

The ferries of today that go to these islands, along with those leaving from Portsmouth to the Isle of Wight, and other parts of Europe, have greatly improved from the old days when ferry traffic was more like shipping cattle from one island to the next, in cramped conditions, with standing room only. It was nothing close to the luxury of today's ferries, and this is probably the reason why many people from Europe and the UK take the ferry route and their cars, with a fast system of getting on and off with minimum delay, to get to their place of destination.

On one visit to Jersey we went to the famous pearl factory, which was eye-catching the minute one entered the building. Never before had I seen so many beautiful pearls and exquisite pieces of jewellery; it was hard to know from which to choose. Finally after examining many pieces, I selected a three-row strand of pearls, with matching earrings, which William insisted on buying for me. I was delighted.

Another trip we did together was to Bilbao, Northern Spain in the Basque Province, 200 miles north-northeast of Madrid, known to have rich iron mines nearby. These have made Bilbao and its industrial suburbs one of the chief industrial areas of Spain. Its greatest development has occurred since the 19th century.

Taking the mid-day ferry from Portsmouth to Bilbao was like going on a cattle ship. Chaos occurred in the large departure shed where hundreds of passengers, packed tight, were waiting to board the ferry, amid much shuffling and groans, due to lack of air and space. William and I milled along with the crowd, feeling more and more like a pack of dogs ready to lunged forward, the minute orders were given to board.

Once aboard the ferry, a crew member showed us to our cabin which was small but comfortable, and I was pleased to notice we had a porthole from which to look out. As we settled in and the ferry glided its way out of the dock William suggested a cool drink, which I was more than happy to accept, after the long wait in the departure shed at Portsmouth. Knowing he had been on this trip before, I asked him if it would be a calm cruise.

Casually, in typical Navy style, he said, 'We'll be fine once we pass the Bay of Biscay.'

Thoughtfully looking at him, I asked, 'What then?' feeling somewhat ignorant of the laws of the sea.

'The Bay gets a bit rough,' was his response, 'but we'll be okay, so don't worry.'

Feeling somewhat reassured I continued with my drink, then we ambled over the ship to discover what entertainment it had to offer. After dinner we took in a night show, then headed for our cabin. I was hardly in bed when I felt the ship begin to roll, my stomach going with it, while we could hear mountainous waves crashing against her side. The noise was deafening and to make matters worse, the cars parked on the upper deck sounded as though they had loosened from their chains and were banging against each other.

I whispered to William, 'Did you hear that?' With the words hardly

William on the right in Singapore, 1961.

out of my mouth and the next crash hitting the side of the ship, I had visions of us capsizing and all passengers being tossed overboard, as casual as a bag of garbage. Still feeling nauseated, with my stomach flying in all directions, I groaned, 'When will it stop?'

'Go to sleep, it will have subsided by the morning,' was his reply. 'You'll feel better, then.'

Hardly convinced this would be the case, I continued listening to the cars banging against each other and the crashing of the waves against the side of the ship, with thoughts of water pouring through the porthole.

When I whispered to my sailor brother could this possibly happen, he assured me the porthole was securely locked and that once we passed the Bay, the ship will be on a steady roll.

Next morning, true to his word, everything outside appeared calm and all I could hear was the gentle lapping of the waves against the ship. Peeking through the porthole, the sun was shining and having passed the Bay, it seemed we would have a smooth cruise until reaching Bilbao.

Once dressed we headed into the restaurant for a good breakfast, with anticipation of enjoying a relaxed day.

Finally docking at the Port of Bilbao we boarded a coach and our driver, who was also our guide, took us literally on a root-march round the City, hoping to show us as much as possible throughout our short visit. Driving through the outskirts of Bilbao one sees many highrise apartment buildings over which hang masses of laundry, giving the impression of a poor neighbourhood. No doubt, many of its residents work in the suburban areas of the iron and steel industries.

The City of Bilbao boasts two Gothic churches from the 14th and 15th century, and the one we visited had beautiful stained-glass windows. The woodwork within is in remarkable condition, as though treated with extreme care, but upon entering the church the mustiness of wood is overpowering. After seeing the baroque town hall, our driver then took us to what was once a military courtyard and it was here, we were told, that General Franco kept his wine cellars. No longer used as a military base, the upper floors of the courtyard are now luxurious apartments, brightly painted on the outside. Before leaving the city, we stopped in at one of the cafe's for a snack and good hot coffee.

Thanking our driver for an interesting tour we headed back on the coach to Bilbao Port. Although we passed the Bay of Biscay on our return trip to Portsmouth, for some reason, I didn't have the same concern coming back as I did going. The ocean appeared calmer and the ship seemed to glide smoothly over the waves, unlike the rough and tumble of before. Perhaps it was the unknown that had amplified my fear.

When visiting Weymouth, William hired a taxi to take us from Hampshire to Dorset. Halfway through the journey, we stopped at a pub. This gave our taxi driver a chance to rest and enjoy a soft drink, while William would down a beer followed by whisky, which apparently gave him a sense of well-being. I usually asked for sherry, but was appalled by the pittance size of the drink, compared to the price charged. However, I did not relate those thoughts to William, as my facial expression conveyed all.

We had been a few days in Weymouth, William catching up with his old friend Bill, with whom he played snooker on Wednesday afternoon, while I did some local shopping. In the early hours of Thursday morning he awoke complaining of chest pains and shortness of breath. I immediately phoned the hotel night porter, who rang for an ambulance. I dressed hurriedly, put a robe round William, who was escorted by two paramedics into the ambulance and sat in the back worried sick out of my mind, hoping against hope, it was not serious. The journey to the hospital left me wondering where the driver was taking us, as we seemed to be hours in the ambulance and when I questioned where we were going, he replied, 'Dorchester.'

'Dear, God,' I muttered, 'what are we doing in Dorchester?' Were there no hospitals in Weymouth, which was miles away?

When the ambulance pulled up outside the hospital, a nurse came out to assist the paramedics. William was put into a small room. I sat in a chair by the side of the bed and held his hand. It was 4 a.m. when the call was made to the night porter, less than an hour to reach the hospital; we waited till seven o'clock before a doctor came in to examine my brother. By this time, knowing the urgency of his complaint, I was seething mad with rage for the lack of care and attention at this hospital, and the time it took for a doctor to appear. 'Surely, a night doctor is always on call,' so I thought!

The rest of my holiday in Weymouth was spent going back and forth to the hospital in Dorchester to make sure William had everything he needed. At the same time my concern was not only for him but because I had left most of my luggage at his home in Hampshire, including my Canadian passport, I was anxious to claim my possessions for my trip back to Canada.

Speaking with the doctor, looking after him, I asked when William could return home but his response was that because my brother had an angina attack, he did not recommend him leaving the hospital for some time. I spoke with his friend Bill about the doctor's prognosis, explaining concern for his health, and that we needed to get back to Hampshire.

Above: William in Waterlooville, Hampshire.

William holding 'Pip" Poodle with Caroline, California 1980s.

Below: William and Caroline with his three grandchildren.

Without hesitation Bill offered to pick up William at the hospital, with his doctor's approval regarding these arrangements, and drive both of us back to Hampshire. Reluctantly, the doctor agreed, providing we stop several times throughout the journey to rest. He also recommended that William see his own doctor, at the earliest opportunity.

Arriving at his home I could see the strain on William's face and knew he was suffering, not only from the nagging pain in his right side, but also from the angina attack. Our friend brought up the luggage; I made tea, and we both suggested to my brother a rest in bed. Once he was settled, I telephoned his doctor who said he would see my brother in the morning.

When the doctor arrived the following day, I noticed he was young, tall and slender. Explaining briefly to him what happened to William at the Crown Hotel in Weymouth, the doctor listened quietly. After he examined William, the doctor recommended he go back into the hospital as he was not happy with his condition, particularly as it appeared the pain in his side could be the result of pneumonia. On leaving, he handed me a prescription to be filled and said, 'I'll look in tomorrow.'

Returning the next day the doctor told me to have William ready by noon, so that the ambulance could take him to St. Mary's hospital in Portsmouth. Getting to and from the hospital by bus in Waterlooville to Portsmouth was time-consuming and tiring; it seemed I hardly got there when it was time to turn round and run for the bus back to Waterlooville, where William lived. Daily visits to him showed some improvement in his health, although the pain in his side still bothered him. I telephoned Rowland with the news that William was in hospital and he decided to visit him, along with his daughter. Picking me up in Waterlooville they drove there and back to the hospital, which practically took up the whole day.

My return to Canada was drawing ever closer; I was anxious to see William back in his own home before I left. Thankfully, after a few days of treatment he was allowed to leave the hospital, with an urgent note to see his own doctor as soon as possible.

In September 2006, on the day of my departure, I left Hampshire with a heavy heart. Instinct told me this was our last farewell. Although I planned another trip next spring I knew it would not happen, as I was aware that William's health was declining and regardless of what treatment he received for the on-going pain in his right side, nothing seemed to work to reduce the agony. He had completely lost the sight in one eye and although he wore glasses, still could not see clearly in the other eye, which left him angry and frustrated. Seeing him this way saddened me, knowing how much he loved life and to even try writing out a bookie's slip was now too much for him.

Our hour-long Sunday chats wherein we exchanged news about all and sundry, including the latest horse racing events, came to an abrupt end when William had a fatal heart attack in his home in March 2007, and was taken to Queen Alexandra's hospital in Portsmouth, where he died shortly after.

For many years William tried to get recognition and compensation from the British Government for damage to his health when he served in the Navy, without success. In 2005 he was notified, in writing, that claims were being made against an American company who manufactured asbestos, a hazardous material to one's health, that was used throughout the ships to insulate pipes. There is no question that working in this environment caused him to suffer with many medical problems. Completing all paperwork for compensation, William passed away before the case was settled in court.

I did not attend his funeral but understand he was given a hero's farewell with the Union Jack flag spread over his coffin, on top of which were placed his Naval medals, well-earned because of his lengthy service in the Royal Navy. According to his wishes, his ashes were laid to rest beside his late wife, Violet, in Winchester. William would have been chuffed to know of the elaborate preparations made for his funeral and equally delighted to think that, in death, he was worth it.

I miss his buoyant chats, Navy humour that would have you laughing silly and rolling off a chair, if you were sitting in one. His gambling tricks in picking silly-named horses that won races, much to the chagrin of the bookies, whose money he spent on gambling, rather than his own.... His generosity to his sisters, and family, was never-ending.

Grocery shopping with him at Asda in Waterlooville, was quite an experience. Like Rowland, he would suddenly do the disappearing act on me and when I finally caught up with him, he would be chatting and laughing to a couple of women. They all knew him at the supermarket and sometimes when shopping with him, I'd hear remarks: 'Oh, here he comes, our blissful sailor.'

Whenever I phoned him, he responded briskly: 'City desk, Marshall speaking.'

I'm sure he thought he was back in the Navy giving orders to the ratings. This system of responding to a telephone call always had me laughing and when the doctor rang it probably had him wondering if he had dialed the wrong number. Like the rest of us, he always heard, 'City desk, Marshall speaking.'

William, decidedly, was his own man, charismatic, and did not shy away from the person he wanted to be, no matter with whom he came in contact. Direct to the point of no fuss, that and his humour, is how I will remember my younger brother, whom I loved dearly.

My two brothers, Rowland and William, who gave love so freely, created a close-knit bond unknown in most families. Kathleen, Elizabeth and I were lucky to be their sisters.

KATHLEEN: A STYLISH LADY 1921-2008

She was four years older than me, and we were different as chalk and cheese. One might wonder why the characteristics of two sisters were so unlike each other but in all probability this was due to the fact that while we came from the same mother, we had different fathers. It would take me many years to determine these characteristic differences and frankly what I discovered, didn't exactly please me.

While we were growing up in the orphanage it wasn't until I reached the age of eight that I became aware we were sisters and that Kathleen's surname had been changed from Brandon to Marshall. The powers that be under whose care we were placed, from childhood, refused to utter a word how or why this came about. No records are available when this change of name was made. In later years, this would create untold misery for her when she wished to re-emigrate into Canada, unsuccessfully. Did my mother marry a man named Brandon, then divorce him and marry my father? What was the history involving this liaison that seemed to grind itself into the ground, and want to hide?

Many years later when researching the family's history we would discover the truth as records revealed Kathleen's father was indeed John Brandon, born in Dublin in 1890. From the start, I sensed an anger and noticeable resentment in Kathleen, that did not bode well with Rowland,

William, Elizabeth or myself, about the fact that we were step-sisters. I tried to put aside our differences and to accept her as family, but there was always a shadow of doubt in my mind that any kindness shown to her she would suspect.

When war broke out in 1939, at eighteen years of age, Kathleen was conscripted into war work and because she excelled with the sewing needle, was sent to different aerodromes to repair the damaged wings, then made of fabric, of aircraft returning from dogfights. While working at one aerodrome she met up with an Irish girl named Mabel who came from Waterford, Ireland. The two of them travelled extensively all over England, and lodged together. Barrage balloons made of silk were anchored with wire at strategic points, used as defence against low flying aircraft and to protect targeted areas, especially around the English coast. Being in the right spot at the right time the two girls were able to commandeer the silk when the balloons were hit, and floated to the ground. It was a case of who got there first, in the scramble to get hold of this precious fabric, because it could be used to make underwear.

At some of the lodgings provided to the girls, the food was not only in short supply but badly cooked, with the result one day the girls ended up with severe diarrhea caused by eating bad sausages. For the girls to be laid up and off work for several days meant those able to work having to do more and more overtime, to ensure aircraft were repaired and fit enough in time for further air battles. It was during this convalescent period when the girls were feeling better, they decided to take a stroll into the town of Shrewbury.

Shrewsbury, in Shropshire, 140 miles northwest of London was a Saxon and Norman stronghold, protected by the river on three sides. Its history extends back as far as the year 901. In the early Middle Ages, the town was a centre of the wool trade. Charles Darwin and many other celebrities attended the public school founded in 1551 by Edward VI.

It was in Shrewsbury that Kathleen and Mabel met up with several Canadian soldiers based at a nearby army camp. My sister, now in

Kathleen in Montréal in 1949.

her twenties, met a young soldier named Bill Evans who came from Sherbrooke, Quebec, also in his twenties, slim, good-looking with blond hair. Although my sister had previously met airmen and other soldiers whom she dated from time to time, this soldier made an impression on her with his quiet ways and did not appear to swagger with money like some of the other servicemen.

During the time Bill was stationed near Shrewsbury, he and Kathleen had been courting for some months and when hearing he was soon to be shipped overseas, decided to get married. Before taking this step, however, they needed the permission of his commanding officer. When appearing before him Bill received not only his commanding officer's support but also approval, which allowed him to marry within a few days in a registry office. There being no time for a honeymoon, and Bill now on overseas service, my sister continued working on repairing aircraft wings, travelling to different parts of the country.

As was the case with other war brides who did not see their husbands until arriving in Canada after the war, along with hundreds of them in early 1947, Kathleen boarded a ship from Southampton to Wolfe's Cove, Québec. She then went on by train to Montréal, to be met by her husband's family. The train carrying the war brides and their children were jam-packed and upon reaching Montréal station, the excited women couldn't wait for the train to stop so they could get off and fling themselves into the arms of their waiting husbands. As the train was coming to a halt, in the mad rush to get off, Kathleen was shoved in the back and fell out of the train. She was met by her mother-in-law who looked at her and her bleeding knees and tearful face. But to Kathleen, the torn skin was secondary to the damaged caused to her precious nylon stockings, now frayed at the knees and covered in blood.

To pacify my sister, her mother-in-law did the best to comfort her saying, 'We can buy more stockings, once we're home.'

As my sister was to discover, like many other war brides, conditions in their new homes did not come up to scratch compared to listening to their husbands, at the time they were stationed in England, giving them a glorified rundown of where and how they lived, be it in Canada or the United States. When arriving at Sherbrooke and she met the whole family for the first time, Kathleen was horrified to find they lived in the outback, farming, miles from anywhere, and "mod cons" were few and far between. She knew her husband came from a large family and was interested in hearing her father-in-law originally came from Liverpool, England, but seeing the living conditions, as such, did not appeal to her. 'It was,' she thought, 'going back to the Dark Ages.'

Owning a few acres of land the Evans family kept poultry and had maple trees, the sap from which they boiled into syrup and sold. They also kept supplies of alcohol, processed by themselves, but it was never discovered how or where this was done and by what means. While the womenfolk were aware of the alcohol, it was never made available to them. Before early fall, and the country was deep in snow, the family would take horse and cart into town to get supplies of food, enough to last them through the winter. These supplies of baking ingredients and tinned foods were stored in the kitchen larder, while vegetables were kept in barrels, in the cellar. The realization of this necessity to get in supplies of food made Kathleen aware of the possibility of being snowed in during the long cold winter months. This was not what she envisaged when joining her husband to live on the family farm and the thought of being closed-in did not appeal to her.

While rationing was still enforced in England and did not end until March 1949, Kathleen didn't quite bargain for the backward way in which her new family lived. Living on a farm during those years did not give one the luxuries usually afforded by towns and cities. But of course people in many countries were still coping with the after-affects of the war and both men and women trying to get their lives back in order.

When arriving at the farm Mrs. Evans introduced Kathleen to her four sons and three daughters. While the menfolk seemed friendly enough towards her, she sensed an immediate resentment from her sisters-in-law. It would be some months later to learn that prior to joining the army Bill was engaged to a French-Canadian girl and, because of this, my sister's acceptance into the family was strained. No doubt their resentment may have been increased by Bill and Kathleen marrying so quickly after courting a few months, while he served abroad, and the fact none of his family were able to attend his wedding.

The living conditions in the farmhouse were entirely new to my sister who found among other things that when she needed to bath, a tin tub was installed in front of the kitchen fireplace and filled with hot water. However this type of lifestyle was prevalent on farms in England where bathrooms were unheard of, and water supplies came from wells. This

Kathleen with baby Carol, Sherbrooke, Québec.

Below: U.S.A., 1950s.

was also the situation at miners' cottages in Wales where the only way possible to take a bath was by using a tin tub. As I had learned on a visit when staying with family members in South Wales, immediately the miner returned home from the pit he took his bath in a tin tub, in front of a blazing fire. Once clean and dressed, the miner and his wife each took a handle on the side of the tub and carried it outside where they sluiced the dirty water down the drain. The tub was then thoroughly scrubbed, in readiness for the next family member. As bread-winner, no one dared to challenge the miner's position in his household; he took priority with the tub and expected his supper to be placed before him, when he sat at the white-scrubbed kitchen table.

A large Rayburn stove was the main feature in a miner's home, which provided heat and hot water. All cooking was done in big black pots on top of the stove, also a huge kettle was kept constantly on the boil. On either side of the Rayburn were two small oven doors with shelves inside where pies were cooked, and food kept warm. To prevent small children from burning themselves, a large brass fender was put in front of the Rayburn and meticulously polished on a regular basis. What often amused me when being offered breakfast by my hostess, during the cooking process on top of the Rayburn, speckles of black dust would fall from the chimney, landing on eggs and bacon. The smell was so delicious I couldn't resist the meal, neither did I want to offend by refusing to eat it. Without being watched, I politely pushed the black specks to one side of the plate, before tucking in.

On many occasions when taking a bath, Kathleen would look up at the kitchen windows to find herself staring into the amused faces of four men. Asking her mother-in-law if blinds or drapes could be put up, her comment was, 'Don't take any notice of them, they'll soon give up looking at you.'

When mentioning this episode to her husband, he was not unduly concerned and said, 'My brothers meant no harm.'

After receiving no supportive response from either husband or his mother, my sister's one goal was to find a place of their own as quickly as possible, preferably in Montreal, so they could go forward rather than backward, as appeared in the Evans's household.

When they moved into an apartment in Montréal, Bill quickly found work. A month or two later, my sister found herself pregnant. Excited at the thought of having a child, when the birth was due she entered a hospital in Montréal. A daughter was born July of 1948, whom she christened Carol. At two-and-a half months old, when checking on the baby, Kathleen was shocked to find the child had turned blue, and not moving. The verdict was a "crib death."

On Friday of the same week, in mid-September 1948, some cousins called to see if they would like to go swimming, perhaps to take their minds off the death of their daughter. Kathleen refrained, but thought Bill might like to go and enjoy the company with them. While the men were frolicking in the lake she sat on the bank, watching, then to her horror saw her husband suddenly go under the water. When the cousins realized what was happening to Bill they dragged him to the surface and noticed he was suffering with cramp. As they supported him under both arms to carry him to the bank he collapsed and died, in front of his shocked wife.

The autopsy revealed stomach cancer. Could this have been due to tainted alcohol he and his brother made and drank at the farm or, perhaps, caused through his diet when in the Army? Having served his country throughout the war and come safely home, it is ironical a young man of twenty-six should die so young.

Life for Kathleen was like she's been on a roller coaster – suddenly she was unsettled, seemingly disinterested in life itself or how she would cope without a husband. On-going support from the church helped, but the agony of losing both child and husband in one week left her demented. When our family received news of the tragic circumstances we were in shock for days and I felt so badly because we didn't know how to help her bear her grief. William was in Gibraltar at this time; Elizabeth and I, both living in England working to survive. Life, for most of us, seemed an endless worry, I wondered if we would ever get off the ground to lead "normal lives."

Taking the advice of several friends Kathleen enrolled at the Université de Montréal to study accounting, at which she excelled. Since losing Bill, however, her life appeared meaningless, as she drifted from one place to the other. Finally, deciding to leave Canada, with its sad memories, she emigrated to the States in 1950, to begin a fresh life. We were in close touch throughout this transition and although I worried about the state of her mind she assured me that while she could never get over the loss of Bill and the baby, she would try to look after herself. I thought a trip to England might do her good but this suggestion she firmly refused, at least for the time being.

With the passing of their parents, each of the Evans boys was left a parcel of farmland in Sherbrooke. When Kathleen heard the news that Bill's portion had been made over to her, her reaction was that it would be better kept in the family, in his memory. While she could have used the money on the sale of it, this was her decision.

Kathleen's life continued to drift like a lost soul, as she moved from state to state. Gradually, with invitations to parties from the office girls where she worked, she began meeting and dating men considerably older than herself. In Detroit she met a business man who showered her with expensive clothes and jewellery. I thought she might marry him; however, 'the fly in the ointment' was he had two sons the same age as her. The young men did not hide their disapproval so the engagement ended, with Kathleen keeping the diamond ring.

It was sometime in the early sixties when Kathleen visited me in England. We arranged to meet up with her friend Mabel, now living in London, and have tea with her at Lyon's Corner House in Kensington. It would be a chance for catching up with the latest gossip. Interested in buying pure wool sweaters when in England, we shopped in Kensington where Kathleen bought several items. After our goodbyes to Mabel, thinking how well she looked after all these years, we caught the train back to my home in Kent. Before leaving we asked Mabel if she ever

Kathleen looking very stylish in this 1950s photo.

thought of returning to live in Waterford, Ireland; her response, 'when I'm dead.' We presumed by that remark, she wanted to be buried in her home town. Like Elizabeth, Mabel loved London with all its activities, and the two of them frequently met to attend a Catholic service. After the service they would go into a restaurant and enjoy a meal together, chatting ceaselessly, without pausing for breath.

When we arrived home I took a good look at the cashmere sweaters Kathleen bought, at thirty pounds apiece, which I greatly admired. They were soft and warm to the touch and I had visions of being the lucky owner of one like that, one day. In those days it was considered a large sum of money to pay for one item of clothing and the thought of even being able to afford it was far beyond the frays of my slim pockets.

Kathleen loved material things, perhaps to compensate for the loss of her husband and child, whereas our sister Elizabeth did not think these important. When Kathleen spotted something in my wardrobe and she wanted to borrow it, I did not hesitate to say, 'Take it.' If the shoe was on the other foot, however, anything I asked that belonged to her, to loan, was strictly refused. Somehow, this refusal by my older sister never bothered me at the time; my attitude was one of blasé, as I knew this would always be the case.

After staying with me a few days she accepted an invitation from a priest whom she had known since the age of seventeen, to join him with a church group to County Cork, Ireland, specifically, to see the "Blarney Stone," which, when kissed, reputedly endows one with power of invincible eloquence. From the time of losing both husband and child I believe she kept in constant touch with the priest who probably gave her support and comfort during a grieving period, but she never spoke of this. When speaking with me about the proposed trip she was extremely excited, not only because of going to Ireland, but also to finally meet up with the priest whom she had known for years. I sensed, as well, that knowing her father came from Ireland, this visit was more important to her than she would admit.

The journey by train from London, according to Kathleen, was a fiasco, between the clergy and ladies trying to find sleeping accommodation on board the train, amid much giggling as to whom would take the top or lower bunk in the carriage. When the giggling abated and everyone settled down, she finally slept. On wakening the next morning, the group were taken by coach to the village of Blarney, where they kissed the stone.

This visit to Ireland made a deep impression on Kathleen who was determined, at some point in her life, to repeat the journey. I was of the opinion that if she could have uprooted bag and baggage she would do so, and gone to live there.

Moving now to California she met up with several wealthy men with whom she had a strong relationship. One was a professional film photographer, who took gorgeous pictures of her. Still young and good-looking with a yen for stylish clothes and jewellery, she collected not only diamonds, but stocks and shares in oil, insurance, and the Woolworth company, which should have kept her in luxury throughout her life. But this was not to be when, in later years, she wanted to sell the shares and signed over the complete portfolio to a stock broker whom she trusted to get the best possible price for them. A few weeks later when visiting his office to make inquiries, she found this "bent" stock broker had not only left the company but took her portfolio with him, without leaving a forwarding address. Despite making many inquiries of his whereabouts, she was never able to track him down. He seemed to have disappeared into thin air.

Another relationship was with a doctor, who appeared smitten with her. I stayed with Kathleen for a few days and was flabbergasted when this doctor, who was as broad as tall, picked up a large orange off the dining-room table, pips, skin and all, and popped it into his mouth. I thought he would choke but, no, down his gullet it went, leaving me in awe.

When I first met the doctor, I sensed his eyes travelling all over my body and while asking several questions about where I lived and my lifestyle, his eyes continued to roam. I wasn't sure if they were admiring glances, or critical ones. In any event, I didn't let it concern me. Being an Evangelist he did not approve of many things, one being the consumption of alcohol, and attending religious service every Sunday was a must.

Kathleen in the USA in 1960.

After one particular service I attended with Kathleen, we were invited to stay for luncheon prepared by the ladies of the church, which consisted of a healthy diet of beans and salads. I quite enjoyed it! If the women of the congregation were able to get close enough to the doctor, eyes all agog, with all this attention on him, he positively revelled in it. I was amazed at all this adoration placed before him, and could not see what the attraction was all about. He reminded me of a large, hairy monkey.

During this time with Kathleen and the doctor she asked me if I would make some marmalade for them, knowing how I kept up with making preserves and conserves each year when fresh fruit and vegetables were ripe. We decided to take the oranges and lemons off the trees in their garden. Loaded with fruit we got down to the task of peeling, chopping, and sterilizing jam jars. When the marmalade set, it was then put into the warm jars and once cooled off, placed on a shelf in the kitchen cupboard. All was fine until the next day when we heard an almighty crash and, running into the kitchen, found a sticky mess of marmalade and broken glass lying on the floor. The reason didn't hit us for a minute, as we stood there looking at the disaster. Upon checking the shelf inside the cupboard we found it had come off its hinge, perhaps from the weight of the jars, sending everything flying.

Kathleen on holidays in 1961.

Another situation arose during this visit. The doctor invited some cousins of his, mainly Colonels in the US Army, and asked if I would cook the dinner. I was glad of this, as it gave me a chance to do something worthwhile rather than sitting outside in a lounge chair sunning myself. While preparing the meal I was somewhat surprised when my sister handed me a drink of vodka and lime, as I knew the doctor did not approve of alcohol.

'Where did this come from?' I nervously asked.

Depending on her mood swings, my sister had a good sense of

humour and a tipple or two highlighted the merriment which, otherwise, was forbidden by the laws of the church.

'Bought it when shopping,' was the reply.

'But,' I said, 'what about the doctor and his views on drinking?'

'He doesn't know,' she winked, adding, 'I hide it behind the bathroom door.'

I don't think for one minute my sister's drinking habit fooled the doctor and while vodka leaves little evidence of alcohol on the breath, being a doctor he would know liquor was taken by one's behaviour, and hidden somewhere in the house. It didn't take him long to find it. When going into the visitor's bathroom, he stumbled on the bottle behind the door. Approaching Kathleen about his find, she promptly turned round and told the doctor the vodka was mine. The lie did not impress me.

With a dark look on his face, he accused me of defiling the sacraments of his home. I didn't respond to his outburst, although I had a feeling further accusations would be coming my way. I remained silent, knowing I was leaving for home in a couple of days.

After his visitors departed, the doctor thanked me for cooking a good meal and said the last time Kathleen cooked him a chicken she put it on a platter with the breast faced downward, its parson's nose in the air. I wasn't sure what to say, so left him with his thoughts. My sister was within ear-shot of his remark and when I looked at her crestfallen face, I went over and gave her a hug, whispering, 'Doctor or no doctor, he has no finesse, and should know better.'

With this episode behind us, the following day when the doctor told my sister he would be home late that evening, Kathleen decided she would take advantage of his absence and enjoy a musical afternoon of old records of the 1940s and 1950s.

Going into the doctor's study she took the records out of a cupboard and while Kathleen sorted out the most popular songs, I went into the kitchen for glasses of non-alcoholic drinks. We sat on the living-room floor, glass in hand, and soon the pair of us were singing, with legs and hips wriggling side by side, to the rhythm of the music. My sister not only had a good singing voice but was a fantastic dancer. She gyrated all body muscles to the tone and speed of music, and amazed me with her style.

When she put on a record by Chubby Checkers, *'Let's do the Twist,'* we got up from the floor whirling and twirling arms and legs, while singing and laughing our heads off! All inhibitions thrown with careless abandon, out of the window.

'Chattanooga, choo-choo' was a favourite, so after putting the record on the old player, we sat on the floor singing and clapping, with feet tapping to the music, and hips swaying. Suddenly, as though by some instinct, my sister turned her head toward the front door and saw the doctor standing there, listening to us. For how long, we didn't know. Kathleen got up from the floor and walked over to where he was standing. I continued to sit, while finishing a rendition of *'Chattanooga'*, with emphasis on, 'won't you please take me home.' When I finished the doctor gave a weak clap. I returned a weak grin. After helping to put away the records, I decided to go for a long walk, alone.

Shortly after my visit, the doctor received an invitation to attend a medical conference held at Manchester, England and took Kathleen with him. While he was generous to pay her air fare, when they arrived at Manchester he escorted her into a cheap hotel, not far from the conference centre. The rooms were small, and as the hotel did not have a restaurant, Kathleen was forced to go outside for meals in rainy and cold weather. Knowing the doctor was being entertained in style, with good meals provided, this experience of being alone in a cheap hotel for ten days, did not go down well with her.

Later, I was to learn how the doctor had manipulated my sister. When she decided to live with him she knew he was in the process of getting a divorce from his wife, who had borne him six children, and was of the opinion that once the decree nisi was absolute, they would marry. Little did she realize that throughout this process he was corresponding and seeing another woman living in California, whom he wasted no time in marrying once his divorce came through. Not only shocked when hearing the news she was no longer wanted, my sister now found herself homeless.

Telling me how the doctor expected her to unbend to his rules, I was aghast when she said, 'Many times, after leaving his office at the end of the day and seeing the last patient or visiting the hospital, he had hardly stepped over the threshold of his home when his briefcase was thrown abruptly across the hallway, while tearing off his clothes.' She then added, 'The first time this happened, he had me on the floor, before I knew what hit me.'

While I sympathized with her story and the fact he had no further use for her, I was reminded of the old adage, 'Love is blind.' Was it love that blinded her in thinking she was his forever?

In 1989, when this chapter in her life closed she went to live in Sequim, Washington, and being near Victoria, British Columbia, where I now lived on the outskirts of the city, we occasionally visited with each other. Kathleen was still an extremely good-looking woman with a flair for clothing and make-up, which she wore to perfection. Her tiny waistline was the envy of all. Whenever I tried putting on make-up, even using her technique, I always managed to get it wrong.

Despite her lack of culinary skills, even to the point of lifting a saucepan or frying pan, she made up for it with excellent artistic talent when putting a home together. Her eye for detail and colour, with furnishings and interior design, was exceptional. Few could equal her style. When admiring her home, with new furnishings selected by herself, I often praised her results, saying, 'We're all good at something, aren't we?'

Moving to Sequim, she decided to try her hand at painting, using acrylics. Her first attempt lacked depth to her canvass but after much practice, her paintings improved considerably. When seeing one of her pictures I was surprised with her selection of colours and how well trees and branches blended together in an autumn landscape. Painting animals proved more difficult but once she had the knack of brush and style, her canvasses came to life. Considering she had no training in the art of painting, she produced some good work.

While keeping up with her paint brush, she took to buying second-hand pieces of jewellery at the local Thrift shop, which she pulled apart and used the components to redesign necklaces, earrings and brooches. The scrounge was on with family members who no longer had use of old jewellery. She never sold any of her paintings or jewellery but surprised and pleased me one day with a lovely necklace made from ancient beads.

Firmly convinced life with animals was preferable to the human race, she bought two toy poodles, "Pip" and "Squeak" and one ginger tom cat. Commendable, indeed, but I've never seen anyone shower affection on animals the way she did, and were better fed than herself. Because of her love of animals she picked up every stray wherever she found them and if not claimed by the owner, would take them to the pound. One grey, feisty cat she kept for some time.

It was during Rowland's three-months stay with me in 1991, he arranged a week with Kathleen, whom he was to meet for the first time in Sequim. As Kathleen was never keen on cooking, or one to spend hours in the kitchen, the two of them went to dinner at different restaurants, each evening.

One night however, much to Rowland's chagrin, as he was dozing off in bed, suddenly his bedroom door swung open and before he knew what was happening the grey tom landed almost on top of him. Surprised, at first, with this uninvited guest, he looked at the cat in disgust, seized it by the scruff of the neck, then promptly threw it out the front door. Next morning, no word of this nightly invader was mentioned. Upon opening the front door, as though to show an offer of peace, there sat the cat with two dead mice at its feet. When I went into Victoria to pick up Rowland coming off the *Coho* ferry from Port Angeles, he told me what happened with the cat. I roared my head off!

'Did you have a good week in Sequim?' I asked.

All I heard were groans and that it was 'bloody expensive.' Adding, 'What's more I nearly missed the ruddy ferry.'

When Kathleen worked in an office I was never sure how she managed to hold on to the job, as her time-keeping left one gasping for reasons. Time was of no consequence to her and she would not be hurried by anyone. On one visit to her in Sequim, we arrived half an hour late for dinner to her friend's house. Needless to say, when we finally knocked on our hostess's front door, we were politely told, 'Dinner is over.'

Whenever visiting Port Angeles, where the *Coho* docked to let passengers off, Kathleen picked me up. As we drove to her apartment in Sequim, a few miles away, before asking how she was, I emphasized the need to catch a certain ferry back to Victoria, bearing in mind that when the *Coho* docked at the Victoria terminal, my driver would be waiting to take me home. Forever telling me not to rush as I had enough time before the ferry left, she would drive me back from her apartment to catch the *Coho*, with only seconds to spare.

This would leave me exasperated, with the feeling a heart attack was imminent. Time and time again this happened, when finally I said I wouldn't make further trips to Port Angeles and if she wanted to see me, she would have to come to Victoria. However, the desperation of catching the ferry on time continued. When it was necessary to get her back on the *Coho*, bag and baggage were tossed on the back seat of the car, with her seated beside, as she complained: 'What's the hurry?'

Knowing how diligent I am when it comes to being on time for appointments, I'm convinced Kathleen played these tricks purposely on family and friends alike, making us 'dance to her tune,' when trying to be at a certain place, at a certain time.

So she could earn a few extra dollars Kathleen baby-sat cats and dogs in several large homes in the Sequim area, while the owners were off vacationing. At one time when Rowland and I visited her in a large house nearby to a heavily-wooded area, we spotted young deer frolicking about with legs high in the air. We stopped for several minutes watching this classy performance and when the fawns seemingly had finished with the fun, they joined their mother who was standing close by.

One evening Kathleen suggested that we take the owner's dog for a walk. The labrador, with a gentle nature, seemed bent on sending a message to Rowland by rubbing his head on his right leg.

'Good boy,' said Rowland. 'Let's go for a trot.'

As we stepped outside, the air was cool and bracing. We let the dog lead us into unknown territory and noticed we were climbing up paths higher and higher, but had no idea where we were heading. Looking down below we saw the shoreline of a beach, but didn't know the location. For some minutes we stood watching the panoramic view of the bright lights beneath us, and lingered to enjoy the breath-taking scenery. To our consternation, however, we realized our guide dog was nowhere to be seen and we appeared totally lost.

As darkness fell, with the thought of being attacked by some wild creature, I said, 'Perhaps we should get back on the path we came up on, and keep going down. That should take us back to Deer Walk, the road from where we started.'

As we neared some large houses we were stopped in our tracks when a voice shouted, 'Where have you been?'

'Lost' was our response, also, 'we can't find the dog.'

'He came home over an hour ago,' said my sister.

'Well,' I replied, 'if the dog had stayed with us we would have arrived back sooner.'

Patting the dog on the head Rowland muttered, 'You might have seen us on the right track before running off home, old chap.'

Kathleen returned to live in California, in the mid-nineties, where she was more attuned to the weather, as she found Washington cold and damp. She continued looking after animals and the care she gave them was both sincere and remarkable. If a cat or dog was sick she would nurse it until its health improved. The time spent doing this charitable work she gave freely and generously. I admired her. While she had plenty of suitors to choose from, she never remarried.

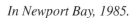
In Newport Bay, 1985.

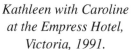
Kathleen with Caroline at the Empress Hotel, Victoria, 1991.

At this time she made the effort to re-emigrate into Canada but was unsuccessful, due to the fact she could not prove the name shown on her birth certificate and the one she gave on her marriage certificate, was of one and the same person. It was most unfortunate because this change of name was not of her doing. But the inability to extract documents that held the key to this mystery, which were not recorded by the authorities who looked after her when a child, made her application to re-emigrate impossible. The complexities of paperwork she was required to fill in by the Canadian government, left her frustrated to the point that she said she didn't care one way or the other and wouldn't go through the hassle placed before her.

I tried helping with the problem but knew it was a hopeless task without the necessary documents, which were never kept by the authorities in England. Had this name change been properly recorded, much anxiety would have been avoided. Also, my sister could have reclaimed her rights as a Canadian citizen and received entitlement to her late husband's pension, if this mess had been sorted out, years ago. But, it wasn't to be.

Her last remaining years were spent in a nursing home. In November of 2008, at the age of 87, she passed away. Hearing of her death saddened me as I felt I could have done more for her during her lifetime. But in my heart I knew that whatever more I offered, would not meet with her approval.

A MAN OF WORDS

An intelligent man, Rowland had a way with words that often surprised me. He had a yen for poetry and although I shared the same interest, for some reason, I could never quite get the right words to convey a meaningful message, or story.

Although at an early age I could rattle off poetry by Longfellow, Keats, Browning and a few others, I did not have the skill to write it. This at times was daunting, as it appeared all too easy for my brother to put pen to paper and turn out a poem with much compassion. Knowing the extent of his thoughts and emotions he put in his writing, often left me tearful.

TO A DEAR SISTER
My life's one ambition, was being with you
The day you appeared, my dreams all came true,
You were all I had hoped for, so long, long ago
Now that you're here, I just want you to know,
Your kindness to me, has made my life complete
No lovelier sister, could one wish to meet,
A deep sense of pride, will remain in my heart
It rebuffs opposition, who would tear us apart.

Your search of a lifetime, rewarded you well
As a tribute to you, dear, your story I'll tell,
In your struggle for truth, so often denied
Dissuade you they'd never, but Oh! How they tried,
Completing a quest, your roots you have found,
With devotion and courage, you seek to astound,
You now reap your harvest, with help from above
And thank him for bringing, one whom you love.

Long years of struggle, have not been in vain
The scars from your battle, will forever remain,
You fought a great fight, overcoming all odds
And challenged authority, posing as gods,
Your long search is over, you have family galore
Now rest on your laurels, on a far distance shore,
The land of your birth, who denied you so long
You now live in a country, where life is a song.

VANCOUVER ISLAND

On the Isle of Vancouver, is where we first met
Such a memorable occasion, I'll never forget,
The moment I saw you, my heart swelled with pride
As you reached out to greet me, with arms open wide.

So alike our mother, with your beautiful smile
I fell into your arms, we embraced for a while
Your kiss was more precious, than silver or gold
You were mine for a moment, to have and to hold.

I will always remember, my days spent with you
So happy together, under skies of bright blue,
On beautiful beaches, of pure golden sand,
Laughing like children, we walked hand in hand.

Those memories remain dear, for as long as I live
Just two happy people, with so much to give,
Reminiscing together, with tales from the past
Fate it was deemed, we should meet here at last.

Oh! Vancouver Island, just to see you once more
With your beautiful forests, that reach to the shore,
To gaze up at bald eagles, as they soar high above
And to walk arm in arm, with someone you love.

On a spring-like day in October 1993, we visited Goldstream Park and watched in amazement the salmon as it neared the end of its journey, upriver, turning from red to pink, grey, then a deathly whitish colour. To begin to comprehend nature at its best in the way it provides salmon with the energy to spawn, breed and then die after the process, leaves one wondering if this isn't nature at its cruelest.

THE MIGHTY SALMON
To rivers cold and crystal clear
Their gleaming water's running fast,
Wherein the mighty salmon's born
Back it comes, to breathe its last.

From oceans vast, they all return
To recreate, before they die,
And multiply, that they may feed
So many folk like you and I.

Upstream in thousands, they arrive
All fighting in their haste,
To seek a place in which to spawn
Until exhausted, lie in waste.

We hear the raucous cry of gulls
With crows he often vies,
To eat the choicest parts, therein
The helpless salmon's eyes.

When scavengers have had their fill
Then nature does its part,
In breaking down the carcasses
That give the young their start.

In river beds where they are born
They lie in wait till spring,
Then leave for waters running deep
Wherein the mighty salmon's king.

THE DAWN CHORUS
Waking each morning by dawn's early light
I gaze up at green trees, with blossom so bright,
The song birds are singing, to greet a new day
I think of you, darling, you're so far away.

I sit by my window and say not a word
Just listen enchanted, to the song of a bird,
The shrill notes of black birds, the lilt of the thrush
 If I only had wings it's to you, dear, I'd rush.

White jacketed magpies, larks warbling on high,
O'er a lovely green meadow sits a brilliant blue sky,
Through lanes as I wander and church bells are rung,
How I longed to be with you when we were both young.

Birds greet me each morning as I rise with the dawn,
The stars disappear as a new day is born,

My thoughts are still with you wherever you are
My darling, you'll always be, my shining star.

Throughout our many months of correspondence I could expect, without fail, in every letter or greeting card some verse or poem written within, which made me feel how compassionate my brother's feelings were when learning he had family in Canada.

ON A DOWNWARD SLOPE

Arriving back in Victoria from our flight at Heathrow, London, I noticed Rowland was unusually tired so suggested he take a rest when we arrived home. While he napped, I unpacked his suitcase. I wondered if the trip there and back was just too much for him and his stay in the Basingstoke Hospital in England for a few days indicated this could be so.

I wasn't feeling that great myself and found the journey from England, more so than ever, exhausting. Arriving at Heathrow Airport hours before our flight took off, plus going through immigration and security, left us tired to the point of frustration with these necessary regulations and procedures. Also, I was concerned about William, with whom I had spent most of my month's holiday visiting in the Dorchester and Portsmouth hospitals.

St. Mary's Hospital in Portsmouth is so old, it must have been built in the dark ages. It is one of the most depressing hospitals I have ever been in, with green walls and cold corridors. To try getting there by public transport is frustrating to the point of wanting to bash one's brain on a brick wall. Missing buses added further concern, because if you arrived late getting to the hospital for visiting hours, it meant begging the nursing staff to let you in.

Once at the hospital I was determined to get in to see William despite rumbles and grumbles that visiting hours were over. I would emphasize, 'I've come all the way from Canada,' with an expression on my face denoting the urgency to see him. This usually worked. While I appreciated the rules of a hospital are unavoidable, in this type of environment the fact that few nurses are available doesn't help improve a patient's healing process

I realized on-going phone calls to William helped lighten my worrisome load, but it still did not take away from me the fact that he was not a well man and lived alone. Although he had family living close by, none appeared willing to look after his daily needs. This did not please me as I knew he cared for them and had given on-going financial help when they were bringing up their young families, for many years.

Rowland, on the other hand, was now experiencing breathing problems, which appeared to be getting worse. He no longer had that spark or energy that kept him running from one end of town to the other, wearing short, shorts, as he did years ago. He was slowing down, as is normal with men of his age. His hearty laughter became less and less and the reason for this no doubt, was due to pain. It saddened me to see this change in him, knowing how vibrant he had been over the years.

My concern for his health was such that I didn't want to think of anything further happening to him, knowing how he had a zest for life and was determined to live it to the full. To Rowland, a missed opportunity was like losing a tooth. Many times we talked of life, how fragile it is, knowing it can be snatched from one's grasp without fully comprehending how this came about. To enjoy life when one is young and to have boundless energy, is one thing, but as we grow older that energy wanes and we find we cannot do the things we once did in our younger days.

We were home a few days when Rowland decided to see his doctor with his breathing problem and to let him know he had been in the Basingstoke Hospital when in England. The doctor sent him for an x-ray, also to have blood work done. When the results of the tests were known

Rowland was advised to go to the hospital where he would need to have the right lung drained of fluid, as this appeared to be the cause of his shortness of breath.

Having this procedure done necessitated a day at the hospital that could take several hours from arrival to leaving, after which time I would pick him up and bring him home.

For a while, removing the fluid from the lung enabled him to breathe more freely, but in a matter of two to three months the problem re-occurred and the procedure would have to be repeated, once again. Although he never complained about these trips to the hospital I sensed that having his lung drained was beginning to take its toll, for despite good results when the procedure was performed, the fact that it never lasted long meant another visit back to the hospital.

The condition with his knees appeared to have settled down, after months of having much fluid taken from them; cortisone shots also seemed to help, making it less of a problem for him to walk without pain.

So that Rowland could have more mobility he decided to purchase a four-wheel walker with two handles to hold onto, also a snap-on-off wire basket used for shopping. This supported him when walking and made his breathing less strenuous. There was a seat on the walker upon which he could stop and sit if he became tired, and when walking was too much for him.

This system of shopping worked well for a while but in his usual gung-ho manner and seeing some elderly people charging round town in small electric-battery-controlled scooters, his impression was that if they could control the mechanisms of a scooter in their golden years so could he, and get around the stores much faster. Believe me, when you saw him coming down the aisle in one, you moved with the speed of a runaway train.

After making a few discreet calls to companies dealing with small scooters, it wasn't long before one appeared on our doorstep. Listening to the salesman give his normal pitch on how the scooter worked, I knew Rowland hardly grasped one word of what the man was saying, as he eyed the scooter possessively. Without second thought, Rowland hopped on the scooter and charged down the road like a March hare, wind blowing round his ears, laughing his head off!

'Piece of cake,' he shouted, as he careered round one corner to the next, holding tight on the handles. 'I'll take it.'

I think he thought he had finally achieved blissful freedom, throwing caution to the wind, with his new toy. Never one to procrastinate whenever a decision arose, he believed in dealing with it on the spot!

Once Rowland had his scooter there was no holding him back. Secretly, this new vigor was hard not to enjoy. I could see what it meant to him by having wheels that could take him from one end of the pier back into town and allow him to chatter ceaselessly homeward-bound, to all and sundry. What I did not bargain for however was that when we shopped together and Rowland was on his scooter, I usually ended up running alongside him, trying to catch up, while he merrily went on his way.

Exhausted, to the point of fatigue, I said to him, 'If you want to go ahead, I'll see you there,' indicating to the store where we would meet.

Although this catch-up was a way to lose the extra pounds of weight I carried, it simply was not my cup of tea. By the time I reached the store, minutes later, I would find him chatting to a complete stranger, also on a scooter, probably comparing notes. One way of recognizing Rowland's scooter was by a long rod attached to the back of it, on which hung a small Canadian flag. However, as there appeared to be many seniors on scooters with the same type of flag, one had to check the man first to make sure you were speaking with the right owner. Once or twice, I got it wrong!

Despite my constant reminders to my brother that jumping curbs on a scooter could prove disastrous, he tried it several times. 'Not me,' came the cheeky reply, 'tipping will never happen.'

But it did!

I would preach, 'If you want to stay alive, you can't keep throwing caution to the wind.' I'm not sure he ever heard me.

Once, when sitting on the scooter, he tried reaching the front door handle to enter the condominium, and wobbled off it. Thankfully, a woman who knew him and saw what happened picked him up, along with the scooter, which also took a tumble, and let him through the front door, dragging the scooter behind her. Luck was not, however, on his side this time. When I saw the extent of the injury on his right leg, with blood oozing from it, I called the ambulance. The skin was so badly torn, the leg required twenty-five stitches.

When his nurse came in two or three times a week to dress the wound, Rowland would chatter to her ceaselessly, rambling on about life in the Merchant Service. Generous, as always, when Christmas rolled round he presented her with a gift, much to her delight! He never failed to appreciate the home service by the nursing profession and indicated how lucky he was to receive excellent attention. One hears of patients falling for their nurses; secretly, I felt this to be the case with Rowland.

The build-up of fluid in Rowland's right lung continued and required to be drained at different intervals. At one time when this procedure was done at the local hospital and a decision was made to keep him in for a few days, he unfortunately picked up a virus and was transferred to the Jubilee Hospital in Victoria. I was aghast, when visiting him a day later, to see that he was in a room isolated from the other patients and no one was allowed in, without wearing a mask and white gown.

Before he was due to go home from the hospital I took the opportunity to speak with one of the doctors who treated him. During our conversation the doctor said they were puzzled with Rowland's condition and could not understand the reason why his right lung continued to build up with fluid, as nothing showed up in his x-rays.

I asked the doctor if it could be the oil ingested when Rowland's ship was blown up during World War Two in 1942, when he was forced to dive overboard into the ocean and swim among oil and debris.

The doctor replied, 'I don't think so, because if this had been the case, the condition would have reared its head thirty years ago, not sixty years later,' but, he added, 'we will keep an eye on him, as there has to be a reason and I'm sure we will find it.'

Feeling somewhat reassured after speaking with the doctor, we left the hospital to return home. On our return, I made Rowland as comfortable as possible; meanwhile, my thoughts were with William back in Hampshire, hoping he had a family member looking after him the same way I was looking after Rowland.

Throughout the ensuing months between 2006 to 2007, frequent trips were made to the hospital to have the right lung drained. Whenever a call came through for him to attend either the local hospital or the one in Victoria we realized this would now be part of our lifestyle we could not ignore. Breathing continued to become more difficult and I noticed it was sapping Rowland's energy to the point where he was becoming distraught with his condition. Meanwhile, the hospital doctors were still searching for the cause of the fluid in his right lung but, now, when further x-rays were taken, they showed the left lung with the same problem. Although the doctors were still unable to pinpoint the reason for my brother's condition, Rowland and I continued to be optimistic that one day they would find a cause and be able to treat it.

After hearing from the specialist that Rowland was suffering with a condition known as congestive heart failure, arrangements were made for him to have an oxygen tank installed in his bedroom. I kept hearing the specialist's words: 'There's something there we are missing, but we have yet to find it.' Although he appeared determined to find a cause which so far had eluded him, I admired the specialist's tenacity to get to the bottom of the problem. I hoped that finding it would enable my brother to get the proper treatment, thereby improving his health and lifestyle.

Now that the aid of an oxygen tank was necessary Rowland, reluctantly, made the decision to sell his scooter and go back to using the four-wheel walker. I know losing the scooter was not to his liking but for safety reasons, there was no other choice. Trying to enlighten his heart I said, 'Another senior will appreciate the benefit of it.'

As time went on and life continued at a slower pace, I found it strenuous to keep things going between looking after Rowland's appointments either at the hospital or the doctor's office, and at home. Many months later I was to realize the hours of work a caregiver gives freely to a loved one is never enough, despite cutting many corners to try to make life more comfortable. The ultimate struggle within oneself is a feeling of utter hopelessness which in turn leaves a person totally lost in knowing what to do best for the patient.

The oxygen tank in his bedroom was noisy and the heat coming from it, at times, overbearing. Knowing fresh air was essential to my well-being, as well as his, I realized Rowland liked to keep warm, so kept him away from drafts. Once he was settled down on the living-room couch, with the oxygen tank in tow and a lead from it attached to his breathing tube, I took the opportunity of opening his bedroom door to let in the fresh air.

While I was intent of ensuring the lead from the oxygen tank, from the bedroom to the living-room was kept taut, many times I would trip over the lead, almost collapsing into the wall. Often the lead ended up twisted round my ankles; how I didn't end up with serious injuries, I'll never know.

In 2008, it was apparent that neither the scooter or four-wheel walker was of further use to Rowland so in order to get him out for a change of scenery and fresh air, we rented a wheelchair from the local health clinic. This worked well as I was able to push him in and out of stores, also take him down to the fishing pier and along the ocean front, where he could check the number of different sea birds, one of his favourite pastimes, and chat with people he knew. Here, we reminisced of times spent crab and shrimp fishing and watched greedy gulls toward the end of the afternoon, vie for the choicest chunk of fish thrown overboard by the man who worked in the fish market.

With a long rope attached to a large crab net, Rowland with great gusto would throw it into the water. Giving the crabs a chance to bite either from chunks of chicken or sardines out of a tin, we sat in comfort on deck chairs with the anticipation of children on a school outing. After ten to fifteen minutes he pulled the net out of the water and measured each crab carefully, to stay within ocean rules. We returned home with several good ones, also a handful of shrimp.

Taking a large pot from the shed Rowland half-filled it with water and placed it on a propane burner. When the water boiled, crabs and shrimp were unceremoniously thrown into the pot. Cooking this way not only improved the flavor, but also prevented the ocean's smells from permeating inside the house. Waiting for the crabs to be cooked had one's mouth drooling for a meal to be enjoyed.

One sunny afternoon when we decided to go to the fish market to sit, relax and fish for crab, I happened to be leaning over the top of the railing and peered into the water perhaps hoping to see lots of them swimming within our reach, for a quick catch. Taking notice of where my eyes were searching instead of my fingers, absent-mindedly, I put my hand in my right-hand pocket and before I realized what happened my house and car keys slid through an open crack on the deck, into the water.

With a surprised-look, I explained to Rowland my keys were now in the ocean. As though to disbelieve me I detected a wicked grin on his face, but I'm not sure exactly what he was thinking. What made it get bigger was that when I asked him if he could swim in the water and get them for me, laughing he said, 'Oh! I couldn't, the water is freezing.'

'That's alright,' I muttered, showing little concern as possible, 'I know where there is another set.'

I asked him to let me have his house keys so that I could walk to the condominium, close by, and pick up the spare ones, which I kept hung in the hallway closet. I was there and back before Rowland could wink.

Arriving back at the fish market and rattling the keys toward him, feeling somewhat smug, I said, 'Aren't we lucky, we can now drive home.'

I was not unduly worried about the keys being on the ocean floor but one of them belonged to the bank and I did feel it was better in my possession rather than some other person, who fished for crab.

After several days of returning to the fish market in the hope of retrieving the keys, I noticed the sun shining in the water on something that looked like metal. Knowing it was the keys, I drew Rowland's attention to it.

'I'll run up to the nearby hardware store and buy a magnet; that should do the trick,' said he, in a light-hearted manner.

Returning with the magnet he tied it to the end of a long rope and giving it a hefty throw that matched the skill of a Scottish Highlander tossing the caber as a sport, dropped it to where he thought the keys were lodged, but missed the target after several attempts.

By the fourth day at the fish market we were hanging over the railing debating the best way to contact magnet and keys, when a Native lad in his teens watched the performance and asked us if he could try. Rowland handed him the rope and magnet. With eagle eye, and a deft stroke of the wrist, the lad swung the rope high over the railing into the water. After his first attempt, rope and magnet came out of the ocean, minus the keys. Rowland and I watched, surprised! We liked this lad's technique – why hadn't we thought of it.

By this time a small crowd had appeared and watched, curiously, to the goings-on. Undaunted, before making another attempt, the lad seemed to be sizing up distance between him and what he hoped would be an accurate aim on his target, before he hurled the rope once more into the water. With an almighty splash that would frighten the daylight out of any living creature living below, magnet and keys surfaced to the delight of the cheering crowd who clapped and clapped. While watching him draw in rope and magnet with the keys precariously attached, we stood holding our breath, hoping they would not fall off the magnet. Once firmly in his hands, the lad gave a wide grin, and handed them to us.

When the excitement died down and the crowd slowly moved away, we thanked the lad for his effort and slipped a large note into his hand. Added to our excitement, we gave him huge hugs. Although the keys were in the water for several days, it was remarkable only two showed signs of rust.

Our lifestyle continued, but it saddened me to realize Rowland could no longer walk without support and depended solely on wheelchair and oxygen to survive. The happy days of wearing short shorts were seemingly over.

JOURNEY'S END

As 2007 slipped into the past and 2008 was upon us, while I hoped this new year would be happier than the last I knew in my heart that things could only deteriorate further, due to Rowland's health condition. The task of keeping him comfortable with his daily needs was becoming stressful, and I was now beginning to lack the confidence of being able to handle the workload alone.

On a visit to his doctor I mentioned to him how difficult it was to continue keeping things under control in our home, while attending to Rowland's needs, which were essential. After listening, the doctor said he would arrange through the health community services for care workers to come into the home and take some of the workload off me. With the formalities completed, it was agreed a care worker would come in two or three times a week, depending on the urgency of Rowland's needs.

The service provided was good in that the care worker was not only able to bath and dress Rowland but, weather permitting, take him in the wheelchair round the town or to the beach. Although Rowland was a lightweight person, pushing him in a wheelchair was not an easy task for a woman of my age. While I was willing to do anything to make his life better, going up slopes, and getting in and out doors required strong stamina, which sadly I lacked.

Hospitals visits for the lungs to be drained continued. On Rowland's final visit to the Jubilee the specialist said he regretted nothing more could be done, and that there would be no further procedures.

Asking the doctor if he was able to find what he was looking for when checking the latest x-rays, he replied, 'Yes, we found something on the right lung but advise against operating because of Rowland's age.'

When we told him that Rowland used asbestos powder to cover the water boilers when in his father-in-law's greenhouses, the doctor went on to say, 'There isn't much doubt this is the cause of his lung condition.' Adding, 'The use of asbestos can take sixty or more years to surface.'

While the news was not gratifying, patient and doctor now had the answer to the cause they'd been searching over many months.

Rowland had put heart and soul into helping out his father-in-law whom I understand never cracked a smile or had a good word for anyone. Being an insurance manager his one daily aim was to achieve collecting monies from his sales representatives and if there were any shortages, severe reprimand followed.

On first hearing his daughter Gladys wanted to marry a Navy man, her father remarked sarcastically, 'Huh, he's probably got a girl in every port, like most sailors.'

What a way to judge another man without first meeting him, and when he did, his attitude toward Rowland never changed. He was tarred, in the old man's opinion, with the same brush he used for all seamen!

Not to be put off Rowland went ahead with his marriage in 1944 to Gladys and despite leaving periodically to go on overseas duty, he returned home to married bliss.

In 1946, Gladys gave birth to a son who was christened Leslie. Nine years later, in 1955, to the parents' pride and joy, a daughter named Sue was born.

It was at Gladys's request that he helped out with the plants and vegetables in her father's greenhouses, along with Gladys's brother Stan. Stan sadly passed away in his mid-forties, perhaps due to using asbestos. The old man was never one to offer payment for work done on his behalf;

neither was Rowland one to accept payment in return. He did it for the love of his wife and his passion for flowers.

Although working full-time at the Mersey Docks and Harbour Board at Liverpool, Rowland gave his leisure time freely to help Stan in the greenhouses. Ironical, as it seems, for work he gave so ungrudgingly to appease his wife's father, this lung condition was Rowland's legacy.

We continued to take one day at a time; some were good, others not so good. Rowland seemed to require more rest, understandingly so, with his breathing problem, which was all too apparent, while his appetite was less and less, and despite making good homemade lunches and dinners, food was the least thing on his mind. His body wanted to rest. Knowing this was essential, I would leave him either on the bed or tucked in with a warm blanket on the couch in the living-room. When settled down in bed for the night, I would peek into his room to see if he was comfortable. Without disturbing him, I watched him with hands folded saying his prayers, then went quietly back into the living-room.

Looking back over the years, remembering him tucking away into mounds of food either at home or in a restaurant, the days of preparing good meals seemed futile now that his appetite had gone. We reminisced about going into Victoria over a previous Christmas period to look at the lights inside the Empress Hotel and outside the Legislature Buildings, we stopped at three restaurants, on different days, where we ate three turkey dinners. Stuffed to the gills, one might say, but enjoy them, we did! On the celebrated Christmas day, however, the thought of eating another turkey dinner did not appeal to either of us.

Never one to totally give up, however tired, Rowland loved going to the summer Thursday market in Sidney where merchants hoped to sell anything from farm produce to jewellery, and other art work. These walkabouts for local residents, and many visitors within the surrounding areas, swelled Beacon Avenue to the point where people were jostling along with dogs, scooters or buggies, to look at vendor's stalls searching, perhaps, for a bargain. Sometimes we stopped to buy fresh fruit and vegetables from our local farmers but Rowland's passion was music, of which he couldn't get enough.

Making a bee-line to where the music was heard I pushed Rowland along in his wheelchair, and asked the musician to play one of his favourite songs. He loved Spanish and Mexican singers. When the music started Rowland would beam a smile then sing to his heart's content, oblivious to all around, who were enthralled listening to him. Before leaving, he never failed to put a few dollars into the musician's box.

Being a sentimentalist he would listen for hours to Julio Iglesias, Placido Domingo, Patsy Cline, among many others. Music was part of his life; it gave him untold energy, and sparked his very soul. To live without it, was unimaginable.

Every Sunday, during the summer months, a band played on the stand in the centre of Beacon Park. In his wheelchair Rowland listened to the music but would fidget if it was not to his liking. Jazz neither one of us could stand, so if this was the concert of the day we moved on to another part of the walkway and stopped to watch the cormorants, gulls and crows vie for position on top of the posts embedded in the ocean floor.

Having visited many parts of Spain, Rowland picked up much of the language and would often chat in the lingo, when meeting a stranger from that part of the world. He would tell me some outlandish stories of what went on at the various beaches, singing, dancing and drinking. Given the chance, had his wife Gladys survived, I'm sure he would have lived in Spain permanently. When painting such glowing pictures of his numerous trips to different parts of the country, the urge to retrace his footsteps became firmly entrenched in my mind. It made the idea of a visit to Spain more and more appealing and one I should take now, rather than later.

In 2009, after Rowland's death and with his stories very much in my mind, my granddaughter Christine and I flew from Vancouver to Toronto then picked up an overnight flight to Madrid. Arriving at the airport I thought I would die from the heat, as this was the month of August but Christine, in her usual buoyant manner, took it in her stride.

'When we get to the hotel, I'm sure you'll feel fine, after you've rested,' she bubbled.

Staying in Madrid a few days we toured the city, then went by open bus to the royal palace where we stopped for a delectable luncheon. We planned to be doing mostly what tourists do but because of the intense heat of the day, we decided to wait for the evening hours when the temperature would drop, thereby making sight-seeing, shopping and dinner more enjoyable. We spent time shopping for items of linen, shawls and fans; the fact that everything we bought was made in Spain, made it worth the purchase.

We were to find the Spanish people do not dine until eight in the evening, or onward, so appetites wait until the restaurants open. After eleven o'clock the musicians or other performing artists appear on the sidewalks, where crowds gather to sing and dance. For whatever the reason, benches anywhere round the square, or shopping malls, are not to be seen, therefore, one is compelled to stand in the heat watching all and sundry perform their acts, while hopeful the legs will hold out.

Prior to our trip I made contact with Rowland's son whom I knew lived in Valencia, and his grandson Paul who resides with his family in Gibraltar. We arranged to meet them at the hotel on the day of arrival, along with another grandson, Phil, who lives in London, England. Over a three-hour dinner we chatted about family, mostly of Rowland and Gladys, with promises to send photographs of Rowland's years spent in Canada after emigrating. Our meeting with his family was all too short, but remains a treasured memory.

I fully understand why Rowland fell in love with Spain and went there with Gladys as often as possible, to different parts of the country. He talked endlessly about the Balearic Islands and when listening to him it was like something out of a fairytale book, which I couldn't wait to explore. I wasn't disappointed.

Flying out of Madrid to Palma Mallorca for a few days, we stayed at the Barcelo Albatross. Our hotel overlooked the clear, blue waters of the Mediterranean and in the early hours of the evening, we watched albatross flying across the sky. As we enjoyed our evening dinners on the balcony, the slight breeze coming off the water gently caressed our faces, and gave us a feeling of well-being. My thoughts were with Rowland, wishing he could be here with us to enjoy the moment. I'm sure he would have been happy to know I finally made the trip to Spain with granddaughter Christine, and experienced some of the delights he recalled so passionately.

On our last evening in Mallorca we went to a show and watched the flamenco dancers and thoroughly enjoyed the evening, over glasses of good Spanish wine. Sadly, like all good things, our journey of two weeks came to a rapid end.

I returned home with the feeling that I experienced a part of Spain where Rowland had visited many years ago. However, during that period Spanish people were known to wear traditional clothing, which is no longer the case, as they now dressed Western style. The scarves, fans, tablecloths and other linens made by them, mostly hand-stitched, are beautiful.

On Rowland's and my last walk-about at the Thursday market in Sidney, we stopped by the musician's allotted space, to chat and sing, as well as drop a note in his box. We then moved on to a stall that sold lavender sprays, soap, mugs and many other items connected to this wonderful fragrant flower. Rowland asked me if I would like a mug with motifs of lavender on it, which I was delighted to accept. This was his last gift to me.

At 9 a.m. on Monday morning of July 14, 2008, when the care worker arrived and tried to get Rowland up out of bed, he could get no response. I watched silently from the inside of his bedroom door and hesitated to approach the bed, thinking that he needed extra time to get up. Again, trying to get a response, the care worker said he was concerned and that he should contact his office for advice. After making a telephone call he told me his instructions were to ring for an ambulance. When the paramedics arrived, Rowland opened his eyes and, looking at me, asked, 'Who are they?' I told him they were taking him to the hospital so he could be better looked after.

Holding his hand, I promised a visit to him at the hospital as soon as they were able to stabilize his condition, and would bring a friend along with me. When we arrived later in the afternoon, I could not believe what I saw. Rowland was sitting up in bed, with a dinner plate on his lap, smiling, and looking for all the world that hospital was the last place where he should be.

Giving him huge hugs, I examined his dinner plate and remarked how good the food looked. Seeing the expression on my friend's face she looked at me, perhaps wondering what he was doing in hospital in the first place, when suddenly Rowland's vocal chords filled the emergency ward with his rendition of *'Little Boy'*, a song I had never heard him sing before, with arms outstretched. I couldn't believe what I was seeing! It was certainly a dramatic change from this morning's concern, when he appeared at death's door. Now he was euphoric in good health or so, I imagined. What had the hospital given him in his drip-feed to show this remarkable change from lethargy to such energy?

His vocal rendition at an end, the hospital staff gave a clap; I felt elated by this turn of event and hoped within a day or two Rowland would be home from the hospital. Saying our goodbyes I promised I would be back the next day, with positive thoughts of bringing him home.

Then, out of the blue, I received a phone call from the emergency doctor saying Rowland's condition was deteriorating. Somehow, after witnessing Rowland singing with a full heart, I could not accept the doctor's diagnosis and felt that perhaps he had made a mistake.

Visiting him on the Tuesday morning, I found Rowland had been moved from the emergency area into a room and looked comfortable in a bed, near a large window from which to look out. I sat by the bedside and noticed food untouched on a plate.

'Perhaps, he didn't feel like eating today,' I said to myself, to ease my concern.

Asking if he needed anything his response was, 'A cup of tea would be good,' which took me a few minutes to make in the nearby kitchen. We chatted for a while then when his lunch came in I decided to go into the cafeteria for a much-needed snack, as I was fully aware of my own diet being in question, due to eating less food. My visit with him lasted till dinner time at which point I decided to go home, after making sure he was comfortable and resting well.

'Be back tomorrow, and I'll bring some goodies with me,' I said with hugs, as I left the ward.

Returning Wednesday morning to the hospital I sensed Rowland's lack of energy and wondered if, perhaps, he had had a restless night. As promised, I brought in the goodies but he appeared uninterested even to look at them, as I left fruit on his side table, along with his special cookies. Was this the result of what the doctor was trying to relate to me Monday afternoon, when he made the telephone call?

Thursday, I stayed at the hospital all day, and most of the time Rowland wandered in and out of sleep. Holding his hand, I whispered, 'Can I get you anything?' but there was no response. I noticed his breakfast tray on the side table was untouched so obviously he had not been interested in eating. Throughout his in-and-out naps I read the local newspaper, then took a mid-morning break to the cafeteria. The thought of food was not on my mind but I realized if I was to keep up my strength, the stomach needed nourishment.

Making sure he was comfortable I said, 'Goodbye,' adding, 'Back tomorrow, have a good night's sleep.'

The time I left the hospital was 6 p.m. with a driver waiting to take me home. Upon arriving home and stepping out of his vehicle, I screamed in agony. My left thumb was firmly locked in the car door as it closed, with blood spouting heavily on the driveway. The driver seeing the blood quickly opened the door, and my first reaction was that I'd lost my thumb. The good driver then produced a clean white handkerchief and wrapped it gently round the thumb as best he could, then drove in haste back to the hospital, for treatment.

Examining the thumb, the doctor advised a tetanus shot and after cleaning the wound, applied a thin wax liquid, saying, 'This is better than having to put in stitches.' As the thumb healed and the nail turned a rainbow hue, and fell off, it made me realize how lucky I was not to have lost it altogether and that the treatment applied, left no scars.

While I was at the hospital having treatment for my thumb, the urge to dash back to the room and have a last look in on Rowland had the adrenaline flowing, but the day had been long and tiring, so put the idea out of my head.

Seeing Rowland Friday morning, he looked hard at the big bandage on my thumb and asked what happened. I explained briefly about the accident the night before. Staring at me with glassy eyes he softly whispered, 'Be careful, won't you.'

I nodded.

I decided not to stay too long visiting, as I was tired and the thumb ached. Telling him I would be back next day I left on the local bus, to return home.

I had barely reached his room Saturday morning when a doctor, whom I didn't know, walked toward me. Taking me to one side she told me Rowland had had a slight stroke. I went into the room and noticed a remarkable difference in him from the day previous. I was looking at a frail man. As I continued to look at him, sadly reminiscing of all the good times we spent together from the first day we met in 1991, tears swelled in my eyes. I couldn't imagine what my life would be without him. He was a man with a heart larger than life itself, and could see no wrong in anyone.

Visiting for a short time, I returned home with a sense all was not well, and while I did not want to admit he was failing and clung on to the hope he would live and be his old laughing-self again, I knew in my heart he could not survive.

Dragging myself off the bus homeward-bound, feeling utterly

useless, I arrived home to find an invitation from my friend Odette, to dine with her that evening. Sitting at her table, the conversation drifted to Rowland's condition. While I wanted to do justice to my friend's cuisine it was more than I could do to eat as I was choking with emotion, my thoughts going back and forth to Rowland in the hospital, leaving me with a poor appetite.

Although I was doing my best to be a polite guest and listen to what my friend was saying, suddenly our conversation was interrupted by the ringing of the telephone. Odette picked up the receiver and quietly handed it over to me saying, 'It's the hospital.'

Before anyone spoke on the other line, I knew Rowland's life had ended. It was Saturday, July 19, 2008, at 7 p.m. when he passed away. He was 89 years of age.

In accordance with his wishes, Rowland's ashes were returned to England, where he was laid to rest beside his wife Gladys in the Landican Cemetery, Birkenhead, England.

When she was dying, Gladys told him not to grieve, saying, 'There's someone out there who will bring you great joy.' She would have been delighted to know Rowland finally found me, his long-lost sister Caroline, and that we then shared a life of fun and laughter for sixteen years in Canada. Rowland was also to learn from me that he had a younger brother and two other sisters, all brought up without parents. Over the years, although living in different parts of the world, close contact was kept between the siblings. This tight-knit relationship was their security to survival.

Looking back to the similarities that occurred in Rowland's life, and mine, it is interesting to compare. We both married in 1944. In 1955 our daughters were born.

When I was leaving Liverpool for Canada in 1967, Rowland was at the same dock where the *Empress of Canada* left, carrying many new immigrants, little realizing the sister he spent a lifetime searching for, was on this ship. When contacting each other for the first time in 1990 and hearing of the ship's name that I sailed on, the first thing he did was to check the passenger's list. Seeing my name on it, he said, 'left me spellbound.' Not meeting each other till 1991, it goes without saying, was sadly ironic.

William spent many years in the Royal Navy, travelling the same oceans as Rowland, who served in the Merchant Service. Both brothers were conscious of having strong family ties throughout their lives and although they appeared different in nature, many of their characteristics were identical. Rowland forever appearing smartly-dressed as though just having stepped from a salon, well-groomed and loved good clothes. William, on the other hand, hated wearing a tie, unless on special occasions, and wore casual clothes that suited him down to the ground. A zest for living, with jokes galore, gambling on horses and lotteries, is how these two amazing brothers chose to live.

Rowland lost his wife Gladys in August 1990; William's wife Violet passed away in December of that year.

Our sisters Kathleen and Elizabeth were in many ways different in character, at the same time both shared a sense of humour. Kathleen gregarious as ever, sailed along in life as though she hadn't a care in the world. This facade no doubt was to cover up on-going sadness in losing both husband and child in one week. Even with the passing of years, she did not overcome her loss. Because of this, she seemed to fall into one trap after the other, seeking relationships with men that never materialized, beyond the bedroom. It was sad to see her drifting along on an endless ocean, seemingly, with no safe port.

'Why,' she asked me over and over, 'have you managed to keep a man around you all the time, when I can't?'

I did not have the answer.

Elizabeth, so caring, would spend many precious hours with the sick and dying in the hope her prayers would be answered, that they would soon recover.

I don't think she knew the meaning of a bad word, and held in her esteem that all people are good.

As a young adult her one and only interest in the opposite sex was a man of her age, with whom she corresponded from time to time and met on a few occasions. His name was Bernard Mulligan, of medium height, slim and fair hair. The connection with him came about because he and my brother William attended the same school together in Gravesend, Kent. William introduced him to Elizabeth.

Bernard, with a shy disposition, took a liking to Elizabeth and while she reciprocated her feelings toward him, she did not want it to go further, so the relationship stopped there.

One day, I was surprised to receive a letter from Bernard inquiring after Elizabeth, so I wrote back asking if I could see him. We arranged a day to meet at his home in Wimbledon, Surrey, where he lived alone. Our time spent together was good, chatting mostly about Elizabeth and William. I liked Bernard and thought he was a pleasant young man, with a good head on his shoulders. After saying goodbye to him, on my way home my thoughts trailed back to Elizabeth whom I wished had been more interested in pursuing his love for her, but it wasn't to be.

Having lost two brothers and a sister within a period of eighteen months, and the other sister in 1993, I am the last survivor of this extraordinary family who coped with life, dealing with success and failures, without parents.

Our parents left behind a history so bizarre and complex that in trying to unravel the details, it has left family researchers shaking their heads. No longer are there any avenues left to research, to find again perhaps more children born to Caroline Elizabeth Ashby. Yet, the sense and consensus remains, there are more children yet to surface.

It is interesting to note that not only was the first child, Marie Capolongo, born at 182 Westmoreland Road, Walworth in the Sub-district of Newington South, but also Rowland, Elizabeth and myself.

Another point worth noting is that when Elizabeth was born 1927, the father's name is shown as Edward Marshall, and his occupation given as builder's foreman. Edward Rutley Pocock (second husband to

Caroline Elizabeth Ashby) served in the Royal Navy throughout his life and was never in the building trade, so one therefore assumes that Percy E. Martin who was, is the father.

The records show Kathleen and William born in the same hospital in Lambeth, in the Sub-district of Kennington, London.

Copies of three baptismal certificates list Marie Capolongo, William and Caroline, baptized at the Church of the English Martyrs in the Parish of Walworth, with the mother's name recorded.

The Baptisms Register of Kathleen and Elizabeth show them to have been conditionally baptized at the Holy Innocents Church, Orpington, Kent, England. On Elizabeth's certificate the mother's name is recorded as Caroline Marshall; whereas on Kathleen's, the baby's name is recorded as Brandon, and no mother's name is listed.

Within these circumstances one detects the bizarre lifestyle of one woman who covered her tracks so painstakingly, using many aliases, she not only created untold misery to her children, excluding the last three sons by her fourth marriage, but left them struggling for identity and birthright, throughout their lives.

Grieving a loved one, there appears no answer to one's sorrow. When the professionals advise that grieving takes less than six months, I shake my head in disbelief. Words cannot bring back those who are gone, neither can counsel advice make things better.

In every family, or individual, grieving is personal and compassionate, so how does one evaluate how long it takes to overcome their loss when in each case, it is emotionally different? Most of us who have lost loved ones never stop grieving; however, we remember the wonderful, fun times we enjoyed which helps fill a void and, for us, to survive the odds.

EPILOGUE

Rowland was his own man, with a zest for living, like no other. He had a fragmented early life, being raised as an orphan until claimed by his mother at age thirteen. He left for marine training at sixteen. Joining the Merchant Navy at seventeen years of age, taking part in many campaigns during the Second World War and seeing many foreign countries before and after the war, he took a special interest in West Africa and India. Seeing both sides of how the rich and poor lived in these countries left a lasting impression on him.

After leaving the Merchant Navy he joined the Mersey Docks and Harbour Board in Liverpool where he remained until forced to take early retirement, due to a back injury. It was the one and only job he ever held in civilian life.

His marriage of forty-six years to his wife, Gladys, was extraordinarily happy. When she passed away in 1990, he decided to emigrate to Canada and became a citizen in 2005.

He found his sister Caroline when he was 72 years old; then brother and sister decided to live together in Canada for the next 16 years and write their own unique stories, both of which were published by Agio Publishing House of Victoria, B.C.

Rowland's *Luck Was My Companion* relates his experiences during the Second World War and took three years to write. Although he was nearing the end of his life, he managed to find the strength for a book-signing event in May 2008.

Caroline's *Surviving the Shadows* is the true story of a young girl brought up in a strict Catholic environment in the 1920s, and her quest to find family. The book was published in 2009.

In relating the story of my early life to Rowland, told with a full heart, I was able to get some of the demons off my shoulders. Years of not-knowing; and years of knowing that unless all details of the history of this family was fully exposed, there would be "no truth to conquer."

Rowland was a man of compassion who would give, rather than take. He laughed at his own jokes and often said, 'Cry and you cry alone. Laugh, and the world laughs with you.'

He was generous to a fault, especially where his family was concerned. His philosophy could be understood from his insistence that, 'I don't want to be the richest man in the cemetery.'

To his dying day, Rowland loved Canada and said it was a great country. While we explored the Western Regions we hoped one day to travel to Prince Edward Island; time, however, was not on our side, so to compensate we perused all local libraries where we spent hours studying the history of each province.

Rowland's one regret was that he didn't emigrate to Canada years ago. My response: 'What years you enjoyed, are memories forever.'

Life with my brother Rowland was unimaginably happy. His generosity so overpowering, I often wondered if I were living a dream. I never knew what laughter did to the soul until we met, and to awake each morning to a new dawn, knowing the day would be filled with laughter. He was a man with a heart of sunshine; a perfect joy!

ABOUT THE AUTHOR

Caroline Whitehead was born in London, England, and raised in an orphanage in Kent. Throughout her life she has taken a keen interest in politics and at a young age, had ambition to become a politician. Knowing the importance of family life she pushed forward for forty years to discover her brothers' and sisters' identities, overcoming many obstacles so the story could finally be told.

Married in 1944, she emigrated to Canada in 1967 and lived in Ontario, before moving to British Columbia in 1987. Her husband died in 1999. She has one daughter, three grandchildren, two great-grandchildren.

CPSIA information can be obtained
at www.ICGtesting.com
Printed in the USA
BVHW030027111222
653938BV00004B/14